IDENTIFYING THE ANTICHRIST

The Man of Lawlessness and the Mark of the Beast Revealed

Edward D. Andrews

Christian Publishing House
Cambridge, Ohio

Copyright © 2017, 2026 Edward D. Andrews

All rights reserved. Except for brief quotations in articles, other publications, book reviews, and blogs, no part of this book may be reproduced in any manner without prior written permission from the publishers. For information, write, support@christianpublishers.org

IDENTIFYING THE ANTICHRIST: The Man of Lawlessness and the Mark of the Beast Revealed by Edward D. Andrews

ISBN-10: 1945757485

ISBN-13: 978-1945757488

Table of Contents

Preface 6

INTRODUCTION Why Identify the Antichrist? 12

Chapter 1. Antichrist in Scripture: One Coming Figure or Many Present Opponents? 21

Chapter 2. The Antichrist Already at Work: Present Reality and Final Expectation 31

Chapter 3. The Doctrinal Lie of Antichrist: Denying the Christ, the Son, and the Incarnation 41

Chapter 4. Antichrist From Within: Apostasy, Deception, and Hatred of the Faithful 50

Chapter 5. Daniel's Prophetic Pattern: Little Horns, Blasphemous Kings, and the War Against the Holy Ones 61

Chapter 6. The Messiah Opposed: False Christs, Desecration, and the Nations in Rebellion 72

Chapter 7. The Great Apostasy Before the Day of the Lord 83

Chapter 8. The Man of Lawlessness Revealed 93

Chapter 9. The Restrainer and the Mystery of Lawlessness 103

Chapter 10. Lying Signs, Judicial Delusion, and the Doom of the Lawless One 114

Chapter 11. The Beast From the Sea, the Beast From the Earth, and the Image of the Beast 125

Chapter 12. The Mark of the Beast: Worship, Allegiance, and Economic Submission 135

Chapter 13. The Number 666: The Number of a Man and the Meaning of Final Human Rebellion 146

Chapter 14. The Destruction of the Lawless and Beastly Order at Christ's Coming 159

Glossary of Terms 169

Bibliography 191

Edward D. Andrews

Preface

Why This Book Matters

Prophecy has always drawn the attention of serious Bible readers. Men and women want to understand what Jehovah has revealed about the end of the age, the rise of rebellion, the danger of deception, and the final triumph of His Son. Yet prophecy has also been one of the most abused parts of Scripture. Some have turned it into sensationalism. Some have turned it into code-breaking. Some have used it to frighten rather than to strengthen. Others have treated the subject so vaguely that the warnings of Scripture lose their force altogether. This book has been written because neither extreme is faithful. Jehovah did not give prophetic revelation to entertain curiosity or to stir panic. He gave it so that His people would understand the times, recognize the nature of the conflict, remain loyal to Jesus Christ, and endure with confidence until the end.

The subject of the Antichrist, the man of lawlessness, and the mark of the beast has especially suffered from confusion. The word antichrist is often used carelessly, as though every enemy of the faith, every false religion, every political tyrant, and every end-time prophecy must be flattened into one undefined figure. Yet Scripture itself is more precise than that. John uses the term antichrist in a doctrinal sense, speaking of those who deny the truth about Jesus Christ and showing that many antichrists were already active in the apostolic age (1 John 2:18, 22; 4:3; 2 John 7). Paul speaks of the man of lawlessness as the concentrated expression of apostate rebellion exalting itself in the sphere of worship (2 Thess. 2:3-4). Revelation presents the beastly political-religious order, the false prophet, the image, the mark, and the number 666 as the mature anti-God structure demanding allegiance from the world (Rev. 13:1-18). Daniel lays the prophetic groundwork with beastly empires, arrogant rulers, desecration, and war against the holy ones (Dan. 7:2-27; 8:9-25; 11:21-39).

This book therefore begins with a simple conviction: the Bible must be allowed to speak in its own categories. John must define antichrist. Paul must define the man of lawlessness. Daniel must supply the prophetic background. Revelation must unveil the final beastly order in its own symbolic and theological form. When those biblical witnesses are confused, the result is disorder. When they are heard carefully, the result is clarity. The reader will see that Scripture does not present a shapeless mass of unrelated prophecies. It presents a unified conflict between the kingdom of God and the mature rebellion of man energized by Satan, yet expressed through distinguishable persons, powers, and institutions.

The Burden of the Present Study

This book has not been written merely to identify evil. It has been written to expose evil in the light of Christ. The burden of these pages is not fascination with darkness. It is faithfulness to the truth. The church does not need another work that invites endless speculation about headlines, technologies, personalities, and hidden codes while neglecting the doctrinal and worshipful center of the biblical message. The church needs a careful study that answers the right questions. What is antichrist according to Scripture? Does the Bible speak of only one antichrist? What is the relationship between apostasy and the man of lawlessness? How do Daniel and Revelation illuminate one another? Why is the mark of the beast first a matter of worship and allegiance before it becomes a matter of commerce? Why does 666 reveal the character of the beastly order rather than merely invite numerological panic? And above all, how does the whole anti-God order meet its destruction at the appearing of Jesus Christ?

The burden of the book is therefore both doctrinal and pastoral. It is doctrinal because false teaching about Christ stands near the center of the antichristic lie. John says the antichrist is the one who denies that Jesus is the Christ and denies the Father and the Son (1 John 2:22-23). He says the spirit of antichrist refuses to confess Jesus Christ as having come in the flesh (1 John 4:2-3; 2 John 7). That means the conflict is not first political. It is theological. Wherever the truth about the Son of God is denied, antichristic rebellion is already at work. Yet the burden is also pastoral, because these truths are not revealed for scholars alone. They are revealed so that believers will not be deceived, shaken, or spiritually disarmed. Paul wrote to the Thessalonians so they would not be quickly unsettled. John wrote so believers would test the spirits. Jesus warned His disciples beforehand so they would not be misled by false christs and false prophets (Matt. 24:4-5, 11, 24). Prophecy serves perseverance.

This is why the book repeatedly returns to the difference between true biblical Christianity and mere outward profession. The greatest danger does not come only from obvious unbelief outside the visible sphere of religion. It also comes from apostasy, false teaching, defection from apostolic truth, and the self-exalting claims of those who stand within the professing sphere while corrupting it from within. "They went out from us, but they were not of us," John says (1 John 2:19). Paul warns that the apostasy must come first (2 Thess. 2:3). Peter warns of false teachers arising among the people (2 Pet. 2:1). Jude warns of ungodly men who creep in unnoticed (Jude 4). This book has therefore been written with a sober awareness that the anti-God order often grows near holy things before it is fully exposed.

The Method Followed in These Pages

A book on this subject must be governed by method, or it will quickly collapse into confusion. The method followed here is the historical-grammatical reading of Scripture, attentive to context, vocabulary, prophetic development, and the internal unity of the biblical witness. The Bible is not treated as a loose collection of mystical fragments waiting to be attached to current events by imagination. It is treated as the inspired, inerrant, and infallible Word of God. The prophets, Jesus, the apostles, and Revelation speak in harmony, though not without distinction. Their categories must be preserved.

For that reason, the chapters move in a deliberate order. The study begins with John's doctrine of antichrist because only John uses the term. From there it moves to the apostolic-age reality of antichrist already at work, then to the doctrinal lie at antichrist's center, and then to apostasy and deception arising from within the professing sphere. After that, the book turns to Daniel, where beastly empire, little horns, self-exalting kings, and war against the holy ones establish the prophetic pattern that later revelation develops. Jesus' warnings about false christs, desecration, and the rage of the nations then bridge Daniel to Paul and Revelation. Only after those foundations are laid does the study turn to the great apostasy, the man of lawlessness, the restrainer, lying signs and wonders, the beast from the sea, the beast from the earth, the image, the mark, and the number 666.

That order matters. If the reader begins with 666 or with modern speculation about the mark, he will likely lose the biblical center. If he begins with John, Daniel, Jesus, and Paul, Revelation becomes far clearer. The mark is then seen as a sign of allegiance, not merely a gadget. The number 666 is seen as the mature number of man in rebellion, not merely a sensational cipher. The beast is seen as the final anti-God political-religious order, not merely any one passing government. And the lawless one is seen as the concentrated expression of institutionalized apostate rebellion, not merely a detached political tyrant. This book therefore seeks clarity by honoring biblical order.

The method also rejects one common mistake that has done much damage: collapsing all prophetic enemies into one simple label. Scripture is more exact. The dragon is not the beast. The beast from the sea is not the beast from the earth. The image is not the same as the mark. The mark is not identical with the number, though it is tied to it. Antichrist is not a careless synonym for every hostile figure in prophecy. The man of lawlessness, the beast, the false prophet, and the antichristic principle are related, but they are not interchangeable in a careless sense. Distinguishing these matters does not weaken the unity of Scripture. It preserves it.

What the Reader Should Expect

The reader should expect this book to be direct. The chapters will not pursue the fashionable habit of softening hard biblical lines. Where Scripture warns, the book will warn. Where Scripture distinguishes truth from falsehood, the book will distinguish. Where Scripture exposes apostasy, false teaching, and idolatrous power, the book will not rename them with harmless language. The biblical conflict is real. There are many antichrists. There is a great apostasy. There is a man of lawlessness. There is a beastly order that demands allegiance. There is a mark that signifies belonging to that order. There is a number that interprets the whole order as man in climactic rebellion. And there is coming judgment upon all who refuse the truth and take pleasure in unrighteousness (2 Thess. 2:10-12; Rev. 14:9-11).

At the same time, the reader should expect the book to keep returning to the triumph of Christ. Prophecy is not given to leave the church staring into darkness. It is given so the church may see darkness judged by the returning King. The lawless one is revealed, but Christ destroys him with the breath of His mouth and the appearance of His coming (2 Thess. 2:8). The kings of the earth gather against the Lamb, but the Lamb conquers them because He is Lord of lords and King of kings (Rev. 17:14). The beast and the false prophet are cast into the lake of fire (Rev. 19:20). The devil who deceived them is thrown into final judgment (Rev. 20:10). The kingdom is given to the holy ones of the Most High (Dan. 7:26-27). This is why the final chapter of the book ends with Christ's victory rather than with the beast's number. The last word belongs to Jesus Christ.

The reader should also expect this study to be pastoral in tone. These subjects are not remote. They concern the church's present need for discernment. The spirit of antichrist was already in the world in the apostolic age. The mystery of lawlessness was already at work. False prophets had already gone out into the world. Those realities have not disappeared. The church in every age must test the spirits, remain in the teaching of Christ, reject the lie, and refuse every anti-God claim upon thought, worship, and action. The relevance of the subject is therefore immediate. The aim is not to produce prophetic hobbyists, but steadfast Christians.

A Final Word Before the Chapters Begin

The greatest danger in a study like this is to become preoccupied with the enemy and lose sight of the King. That must not happen. Every chapter that follows is meant to sharpen discernment, but none of them is written so that the reader will leave admiring the complexity of evil. The purpose is to expose evil as temporary, judged, and doomed. The anti-God order may appear powerful, but it is numbered as man, not God. It may gather nations, but the Son will break them with a rod of iron (Ps. 2:9). It may deceive multitudes, but those who love the truth will endure. It may wear down the holy ones for a time, but the kingdom will be given to them under Christ's everlasting reign.

The church now lives in an age when confusion about prophecy is common, confusion about doctrine is widespread, and confusion about the line between true Christianity and outward religion is often cultivated rather than corrected. That makes this subject especially urgent. If believers do not understand the biblical doctrine of antichrist, they will not recognize how central the truth about Christ really is. If they do not understand apostasy, they will confuse visible religion with faithfulness. If they do not understand the mark and the beast, they will either trivialize the danger or be driven into panic. If they do not understand Christ's final destruction of the whole lawless and beastly order, they will end in fear rather than confidence.

It is my prayer that this book will help the reader see these matters with greater clarity and greater courage. The aim is not novelty. It is faithfulness. The aim is not speculative excitement. It is biblical understanding. The aim is not to make the church fear the future, but to make the church more steadfast in the present because the future belongs to Christ. The anti-God order will rise in its appointed measure. The apostasy will reveal itself. The beastly system will demand loyalty. But Jesus Christ will appear, the lawless one will be destroyed, the beast and the false prophet will be judged, Satan will meet his end, and the kingdom will belong openly to the holy ones under the reign of the victorious Messiah.

With that before us, we now turn to the Scriptures themselves.

Edward D. Andrews

Author of 220+ books and Chief Translator of the Updated American Standard Version (UASV)

Edward D. Andrews

INTRODUCTION Why Identify the Antichrist?

Why This Subject Demands Careful Biblical Attention

The subject of the Antichrist, the man of lawlessness, and the mark of the beast has stirred the minds of Bible readers for centuries. It has also been one of the most confused and abused areas of prophetic study. Some approach the subject with fear and speculation. Others approach it with skepticism and dismissiveness. Still others combine passages carelessly, forcing every prophetic figure into one undefined enemy and reducing the warnings of Scripture to little more than dramatic religious language. None of those approaches does justice to the inspired Word of God. Jehovah did not preserve these prophecies so that His people would be driven into panic, lost in endless code-breaking, or distracted by superficial speculation. He gave them so that His people would understand the nature of the rebellion against His Son, recognize the danger of deception, remain steadfast in the truth, and look with confidence to the triumph of Jesus Christ.

This book has been written because the church must return to the biblical text itself. The only safe ground in a study such as this is the ground of Scripture rightly interpreted. That means we must begin where the Bible begins, define terms as the Bible defines them, distinguish figures that Scripture distinguishes, and connect themes only where Scripture itself gives the connection. The result is far more coherent, far more serious, and far more spiritually useful than the popular confusion that so often surrounds these themes. The Bible does not speak vaguely. It speaks with precision. John speaks of antichrist. Paul speaks of the man of lawlessness. Daniel provides the prophetic pattern of beastly dominion and self-exalting rulers. Revelation unveils the final political-religious order that demands worship and opposes God. These witnesses are not contradictory. They are complementary. But they must be heard in their own categories if we are to understand the truth.

IDENTIFYING THE ANTICHRIST

The burden of the present work is therefore simple and urgent. We must identify the Antichrist in the way Scripture identifies the antichristic reality. We must identify the man of lawlessness in the way Paul presents him. We must identify the beastly order in the way Revelation portrays it. We must identify the mark of the beast as Revelation explains it, not as modern fear imagines it. And in all of this, we must remember that prophecy is never given so that the people of God will become fascinated with evil. Prophecy is given so that the people of God will remain loyal to Christ while evil is exposed, judged, and finally destroyed.

The Confusion That Must Be Corrected

One of the most damaging habits in prophetic teaching has been the tendency to use the word *Antichrist* as a container for nearly everything. Many people hear the word and think immediately of one future political dictator, one hidden world ruler, or one sensational end-time figure who somehow absorbs every passage in Daniel, every warning of Jesus, every statement of Paul, and every symbol in Revelation. That approach is not careful exegesis. It is a flattening of biblical categories. The New Testament itself does not use the term in that careless way. In fact, the word *antichrist* appears only in John's letters, and John uses it in a definitional and doctrinal context. He speaks of many antichrists already active in his own day. He says the spirit of antichrist was already in the world. He identifies antichrist by denial of the truth about Jesus Christ, by departure from apostolic truth, and by refusal to confess the Son properly.

That alone should change the way the subject is approached. The first question is not, "Which modern public figure is the Antichrist?" The first question is, "What does Scripture mean by antichrist?" John's answer is unmistakable. Antichrist is not first a matter of political branding or technological control. It is first a matter of doctrinal rebellion against Jesus Christ. The antichristic lie denies that Jesus is the Christ, denies the Father and the Son, and refuses to confess Jesus Christ as having come in the flesh. That means the heart of the conflict is theological before it becomes imperial, social, or economic. Any study that loses that center has already left the apostolic foundation.

At the same time, this book will show that John's doctrine of antichrist is not isolated from the wider prophetic witness. Daniel describes beastly empire, arrogant rulers, desecration, and war against the holy ones. Jesus warns of false christs, false prophets, desecrating rebellion, and hatred against His followers. Paul speaks of the apostasy and the man of lawlessness. Revelation presents the dragon, the beast from the sea, the beast from the earth, the image of the beast, the mark, and the number 666. These are not disconnected themes. They belong to one broad biblical conflict between the kingdom of God and the mature anti-God order. Yet they are not all identical in a simplistic sense. This book has been written to preserve both the unity and the distinctions.

The Central Question of the Book

The title of this book includes three linked ideas: the Antichrist, the man of lawlessness, and the mark of the beast. Each of these is important, but each must be handled according to its own biblical setting. The Antichrist must be understood from John's letters. The man of lawlessness must be understood from 2 Thessalonians 2. The mark of the beast must be understood from Revelation 13 and the surrounding context. The central question is not whether these themes are related. They clearly are. The central question is how they are related without confusion, contradiction, or careless collapse.

The answer advanced in these pages is that Scripture presents a unified antichristic conflict that takes different but related forms. John reveals the doctrinal and spiritual reality already active in many deceivers. Paul reveals the concentrated public expression of apostate lawlessness in the sphere of worship. Daniel supplies the prophetic pattern of arrogant self-exalting dominion. Revelation reveals the mature political-religious order energized by Satan and directed against God, the Lamb, and the holy ones. The mark of the beast is the sign of allegiance to that order in thought and action. The number 666 interprets the whole beastly structure as man in intensified rebellion, falling short of divine fullness while claiming false greatness.

This approach matters because it protects the reader from false simplification. The Bible is not less coherent than popular prophecy; it is more coherent. The problem is not that Scripture is confused. The problem is that interpreters often begin with assumptions imported from outside the text. Once the text is allowed to govern, the matter becomes clearer. John does not speak the way later sensationalism often speaks. Paul does not speak the way modern speculation often speaks. Revelation does not support the shallow reduction of the mark to one isolated technological fear detached from worship. Scripture gives a richer, more sobering, and more theologically profound account.

The Conflict Is First About Christ

At the center of all these prophecies stands Jesus Christ. That truth must be stated plainly at the outset because many discussions of these themes drift into a strange imbalance. Men become so absorbed in the beast, the mark, and the final rebellion that they forget the conflict is fundamentally about the Son of God. The nations rage against Jehovah and against His Anointed. False christs arise to mislead many. Antichrist denies that Jesus is the Christ and denies the Father and the Son. The man of lawlessness exalts himself in the sphere that belongs to God. The beast demands worship that belongs only to God and the Lamb. The mark signifies allegiance to an anti-God order. Every strand of the rebellion is therefore anti-Christ in the deepest sense because every strand seeks to displace, deny, counterfeit, or oppose the rightful supremacy of Jesus Christ.

That means the conflict is never merely about public events. It is about worship. It is about truth. It is about loyalty. It is about who has the right to rule the conscience, command the life, and receive the devotion of mankind. Revelation makes this especially clear. The beast is not content with political influence. It seeks worship. The false prophet is not merely an assistant to civil power. It is a religious deceiver that directs men to worship the beast. The image of the beast is not simply a symbolic curiosity. It is institutionalized idolatry. The mark is not first about commerce. It is first about allegiance. Even buying and selling are brought into the service of worshipful submission to the anti-God order. This is why the issue cannot be reduced to world events alone. The issue is always whether man will remain loyal to Jehovah and to His Christ or bow to rebellious substitutes.

This is also why doctrinal precision about Jesus Christ must be treated as essential rather than optional. Antichrist does not begin when tanks roll or economies shift. Antichrist begins where the truth about Jesus Christ is denied. That is John's burden, and it remains foundational. A false christology is not a minor error. It is theological rebellion. A false doctrine of the Son is not an unfortunate mistake at the edges of religion. It is the lie at the heart of the antichristic spirit. Before a reader can understand the beast or the mark, he must understand why the true identity of Christ stands at the center of the whole conflict.

The Need to Distinguish True Christianity From Mere Profession

Another burden of this book is to separate true biblical Christianity from mere outward profession. This distinction is not harsh. It is biblical. One of the greatest themes in the passages we will examine is that danger arises not only from obvious unbelief outside the professing sphere, but also from apostasy within it. John says, "They went out from us, but they were not of us." Paul warns of a falling away from the faith. He warns elders that men will arise from among themselves speaking twisted things. Peter warns of false teachers among the people. Jude warns of ungodly intruders who creep in unnoticed. The lawless one stands in relation to the temple of God. The beastly order gains power not only by open hostility but also by deceptive religious support.

That means the visible sphere of religion must not be confused with fidelity to God. A person may speak the language of faith and still not love the truth. A body may claim Christian identity and yet depart from apostolic doctrine. A religious office may appear venerable while functioning as part of institutionalized apostasy. A profession may be loud while the heart remains opposed to Christ. These realities are deeply unsettling, but Scripture does not hide them. It exposes them so the faithful will remain in the teaching of Christ and will not be carried away by names, forms, or structures detached from the truth.

This is especially important in the study of the great apostasy and the man of lawlessness. The rebellion Paul describes is not merely the moral decline of secular culture. It is a revolt from revealed truth within the professing sphere. It is religious in character. It is apostate rather than merely pagan. That distinction shapes the whole argument of the book. The final anti-God order is not only a civil structure imposed from outside religion. It is a political-religious order that claims authority in the realm of worship and seeks allegiance in the place that belongs to God. Once this is grasped, many prophetic passages align more clearly.

The Mark of the Beast and the Error of Shallow Interpretation

Among all prophetic themes, few have generated more confusion than the mark of the beast. Many have rushed to identify the mark with some immediate mechanism while detaching it from the worshipful context of Revelation. That mistake must be corrected. Revelation itself places the mark in the context of beast-worship, image-worship, false prophetic deception, and anti-God allegiance. The forehead and hand already carry biblical significance in relation to thought and action, loyalty and obedience. The mark therefore signifies belonging to the beastly order in mind and conduct. It is the beast's counter-covenant sign, standing over against the divine name borne by God's servants.

This does not mean the mark has no practical or public consequences. Revelation clearly says buying and selling become instruments of coercion. But commerce is not the heart of the symbol. Worship is. Allegiance is. Identity is. The anti-God order seeks to claim human beings the way God claims His people. It demands visible conformity. It pressures the conscience. It ties public participation to rebellious loyalty. The mark belongs to that whole structure. To reduce it to a shallow technological theory is to strip the passage of its biblical depth.

The same is true of the number 666. It is not given so that the church will live in numerological panic. It is given so that the church will understand the beastly order as the mature expression of fallen humanity in rebellion. It is "a man's number" because it belongs to man, not God. In the symbolic world of Revelation, it stands over against divine fullness and exposes the beast's pretended greatness as intensified human deficiency. The number interprets the whole order.

It does not merely invite endless code-cracking. This book will therefore treat 666 theologically, not sensationally.

The Triumph of Christ as the Book's Final Horizon

The final reason for this Introduction is to make clear where the book is headed. It is headed toward Christ's triumph. No prophetic study is balanced if it ends with the beast rather than with the Lamb, with 666 rather than with the kingdom, or with the dragon rather than with the reign of God and of His Christ. Scripture never leaves the faithful there. The lawless one is destroyed by the appearance of Christ's coming. The beast and the kings of the earth are conquered by the Lamb, who is Lord of lords and King of kings. The false prophet is thrown into judgment. The devil who deceived the nations meets his final doom. The kingdom is given to the holy ones. The last word belongs to Jesus Christ.

This matters pastorally as much as it does theologically. Many believers approach prophecy with anxiety because they have been trained to think that evil is the main subject and that Christ's victory is little more than a brief epilogue. The Bible teaches the opposite. Evil is exposed so that Christ's victory may be seen in full contrast. Beastly power is temporary. Lawlessness is temporary. Apostasy is temporary. Deception is temporary. Economic coercion is temporary. The kingdom of Christ is not temporary. The rule of the Lamb is everlasting. The inheritance of the holy ones is secure. The enemies rage for a season, but the Son reigns forever.

That is why this Introduction must end by setting the right tone for everything that follows. The chapters ahead will be serious because the warnings of Scripture are serious. They will expose doctrinal lies, apostasy, false religion, beastly power, and final rebellion. But they will do so under the light of Christ's supremacy. The aim is not to produce fear. The aim is fidelity. The aim is not fascination with evil. The aim is steadfastness in the truth. The aim is not sensationalism. The aim is biblical understanding that strengthens the church to endure.

What follows, then, is not an attempt to force prophecy into novelty. It is an attempt to let the whole biblical witness speak clearly. John, Daniel, Jesus, Paul, and Revelation will each be heard in their proper place. Terms will be defined by Scripture. Patterns will be traced carefully. Distinctions will be preserved. The anti-God order will be exposed. And through it all, the reader will be brought again and again to the same certainty: every antichristic power is temporary, judged, and doomed before the victorious Messiah. Jesus Christ is not threatened by the final rebellion. He destroys it. He is not displaced by the beastly order. He judges it. He is not overshadowed by the mark of the beast. He marks His own with His name. He is not rivaled by the kingdoms of this world. He inherits the nations and reigns forever.

With that before us, we are ready to begin.

Edward D. Andrews

Part One: The Johannine Doctrine of Antichrist

Chapter 1. Antichrist in Scripture: One Coming Figure or Many Present Opponents?

The Only New Testament Writer Who Uses the Term Antichrist

Any serious study of this subject must begin with a simple but decisive fact: the term **antichrist** appears only in the letters of John. It is not used by Matthew, Mark, Luke, Paul, Peter, Jude, or even Revelation. That fact does not reduce the importance of other passages that describe false christs, apostasy, the man of lawlessness, or beastly opposition to God. It does mean, however, that if a writer wants to define what *antichrist* means, he must begin where Scripture itself begins—with John. A great deal of confusion has entered prophetic discussion because interpreters have often started somewhere else.

They have begun with later systems, modern speculation, political anxieties, or popular end-time theories, and then forced John's words to fit those prior assumptions. John must not be made to serve definitions that came from outside his own writings. His language is not vague, and his categories are not accidental. He tells the reader plainly what antichrist is, where it appears, how it operates, and why its presence matters.

This observation immediately guards the church from a false start. Many approach the subject with the assumption that the Bible speaks of only one future supervillain called the Antichrist, as though the matter were already settled before the text is opened. Yet when the reader comes to 1 John 2:18, he does not find John saying only that one antichrist will come in the distant future. Instead, he says, "you have heard that antichrist is coming," and then immediately adds, "even now many antichrists have arisen." That sentence alone overturns the simplistic idea that the biblical doctrine of antichrist is exhausted by a single end-time figure. John's wording compels a more careful formulation. There is an expected coming antichristic reality, but there are also already many antichrists. Scripture therefore presents both anticipation and present manifestation. The category is larger than one isolated person, even if it may reach a concentrated final expression later.

The importance of this point cannot be overstated. If the church fails to let John define his own term, it will misidentify the danger. It will look only for one future enemy while overlooking the doctrinal deceivers already active in its own midst. John wrote to protect believers from precisely that blindness. He did not give the word *antichrist* merely to satisfy curiosity about the distant future. He used it as a pastoral warning for the present. He wanted Christians to recognize antichristic activity in real teachers, real defections, real denials, and real assaults on apostolic truth. In that sense, the doctrine of antichrist is not given to feed sensationalism. It is given to sharpen discernment. The church does not honor Scripture by treating antichrist as a speculative puzzle detached from living error. It honors Scripture by hearing John's warning in the very way he delivered it.

John's use of the term also reveals the theological center of the issue. Antichrist is not first defined by military aggression, technological control, or political theater. In John's letters, antichrist is identified first by **false doctrine about Jesus Christ**. That does not mean antichrist has no historical, institutional, or persecuting dimensions. Later chapters will show that evil develops into larger structures of rebellion. But John begins at the doctrinal heart of the matter. He confronts denial of Jesus as the Christ, denial of the Father and the Son, and refusal to confess Jesus Christ as having come in the flesh (1 John 2:22–23; 4:2–3; 2 John 7). From the beginning, then, antichrist is a theological assault before it is anything else. It is rebellion against the truth of the Son of God.

"You Have Heard That Antichrist Is Coming"

John writes to his readers, "Young children, it is the last hour, and just as you have heard that antichrist is coming, even now many antichrists have arisen" (1 John 2:18). His words show that the expectation of antichrist was already part of the teaching they had received. John does not introduce the concept as a novelty. He refers to something they had already heard. That earlier instruction did not arise from folklore or rumor. It arose from the teaching stream established by Christ and His apostles. Jesus Himself warned repeatedly about false christs and false prophets. In Matthew 24:5, He said that many would come in His name, misleading many. In Matthew 24:11, He warned that many false prophets would arise and mislead many. In Matthew 24:24, He stated again that false christs and false prophets would arise and would perform great signs and wonders in an effort to mislead, if possible, even the chosen ones. John's readers had therefore "heard" of coming antichristic deception because the Lord had already warned the church that false messianic pretenders and religious deceivers would appear.

The phrase "antichrist is coming" should not be isolated from that broader teaching. John is not inventing a new prophetic category unrelated to Christ's own warnings. Rather, he is giving a doctrinal name to the same hostile reality. The prefix *anti-* carries the sense of being against Christ and also standing in the place of Christ. Antichrist opposes the true Christ and advances a rival claim that displaces Him. That is exactly what false christs do. They do not merely deny openly; they counterfeit, replace, corrupt, and usurp. They present another message, another authority, another christology, another path, another supposed spiritual center. In that way, antichristic deception is not always blunt atheism. It often wears religious clothing. It often enters through doctrinal distortion, counterfeit spirituality, and departure from apostolic truth while still claiming higher insight.

John's statement also places the church in an atmosphere of urgency. "It is the last hour," he says. Whatever one says about the full chronological scope of that phrase, one fact stands beyond dispute: John did not treat antichrist as a remote concern belonging only to a far-off age. He placed it in the living horizon of the apostolic church. The antichrist expectation was not postponed into irrelevance. The danger had already reached the churches. John's readers were not told merely to file away a prophetic detail for later generations. They were told that the presence of many antichrists confirmed the seriousness of the hour in which they were living. The church had entered a period in which decisive separation between apostolic truth and antichristic falsehood was underway.

This helps explain why John writes with such directness. He does not sound detached, academic, or curious. He writes as a shepherd protecting believers from seduction. In that respect, John's doctrine of antichrist must be read pastorally as well as prophetically. It is a warning designed to keep Christians abiding in what they heard from the beginning (1 John 2:24). The best protection against antichrist is not fascination with evil. It is steadfast adherence to apostolic doctrine concerning Jesus Christ. John does not direct believers to decode headlines. He directs them to remain in the Son and in the Father, to test the spirits, and to reject those who depart from the truth.

"Even Now Many Antichrists Have Arisen"

The force of John's argument lies in the contrast and connection between what was heard and what was now visible. "You have heard that antichrist is coming; even now many antichrists have arisen" (1

John 2:18). This means the church must not think in narrow either-or terms. The future expectation does not cancel the present manifestation, and the present manifestation does not cancel the reality of a more concentrated culmination. John insists that antichrist was already active in his own day through "many antichrists." He therefore gives the church a category that is both historical and theological. Antichrist is not only awaited; it is recognized in present deceivers. The first-century church did not lack evidence. It was seeing the doctrine of antichrist unfolding before its eyes.

John then identifies one obvious mark of these many antichrists: "They went out from us, but they were not of us" (1 John 2:19). This is a crucial statement. Antichrist in John's letters is not merely pagan hostility from outside the visible Christian sphere. It includes apostasy from within the professing community. These individuals had once stood among believers outwardly, but they did not remain in apostolic truth. Their departure revealed their true character. John does not say they were once genuinely grounded in the truth and then innocently drifted. He says their going out demonstrated that they never truly belonged to the apostolic fellowship in the deepest sense. Their separation from faithful teaching made manifest what they really were.

This is where Acts 20:29–30 becomes deeply relevant. Paul warned the Ephesian elders that after his departure savage wolves would come in among them and would not spare the flock, and that from among their own selves men would arise, speaking twisted things, to draw away disciples after themselves. That warning harmonizes perfectly with John's words. Antichristic opposition does not only batter the church from the outside through persecution. It also infiltrates, corrupts, and fractures from within through false teaching. The wolves do not announce themselves honestly as wolves. They arise in connection with the flock. They speak perverse things. They seek followers. They produce departure from apostolic truth. John's "many antichrists" and Paul's "savage wolves" describe the same kind of ecclesial danger from different angles.

John's language also destroys complacency. The church is never safe merely because it has a history, a name, a public structure, or a claim to continuity. If men depart from the apostolic confession of

Christ, they are not neutral variations within the Christian family. John gives them a far more severe name. He calls them antichrists. This severity is necessary because the issue is not a minor doctrinal adjustment. It is rebellion against the truth about the Son. That is why John's readers must learn not to sentimentalize defection. Not everyone who once associated with the congregation remains a friend of the truth. Some leave because they reject the truth they once professed outwardly. When that occurs, the church must call the matter what Scripture calls it.

The Doctrinal Center of Antichrist

John never allows the reader to remain uncertain about the doctrinal essence of antichrist. In 1 John 2:22, he asks, "Who is the liar if not the one denying that Jesus is the Christ?" He then answers, "This is the antichrist, the one denying the Father and the Son." This is one of the clearest definitional statements in Scripture. Antichrist is fundamentally christological falsehood. It is not merely bad behavior, though bad behavior follows from it. It is not merely anti-religious hostility, though hostility grows from it. At its center it is denial of Jesus' true identity and denial of the Father-Son relationship that stands at the heart of divine revelation. Whoever rejects the Son does not have the Father (1 John 2:23). There is no faithful worship of God apart from the true confession of His Son.

That means antichrist is not confined to openly secular systems. It can appear wherever Jesus Christ is misrepresented, diminished, redefined, or denied. John's doctrine cuts through religious camouflage. A movement may speak reverently about God, morality, spirituality, prophecy, ethics, or miracles. If it denies the truth about the Son, John does not classify it as a legitimate variation within godliness. He classifies it as antichristic. This is why the church must never surrender the centrality of right doctrine about Jesus Christ. John 10:36 records Jesus identifying Himself as the One whom the Father sanctified and sent into the world, the Son of God. Luke 9:35 records the Father's own declaration from heaven concerning Jesus: "This is My Son, the One chosen; listen to Him." To deny the Son is to contradict both the Father's testimony and the apostolic witness.

John expands this doctrinal test further in 1 John 4:1–3. Believers are told not to believe every inspired expression, but to test the spirits, because many false prophets have gone out into the world. Every inspired expression that confesses Jesus Christ as having come in the flesh is from God, and every inspired expression that does not confess Jesus is not from God. "This," John says, "is the spirit of the antichrist." Here again John joins doctrinal deviation with spiritual origin. Antichrist is not merely an intellectual error. It is a spiritually charged falsehood opposed to God. The battle is therefore not superficial. It concerns the truth of the incarnation, the identity of the Son, and the saving revelation of God in Christ. To attack those truths is to operate in the sphere of antichrist.

Second John 7 confirms the same point. "Many deceivers have gone out into the world, those not confessing Jesus Christ as coming in the flesh. This is the deceiver and the antichrist." John again joins plurality and singularity. There are "many deceivers," yet he says, "this is the deceiver and the antichrist." The singular form does not erase the many; it gathers them under one recognized character. They are many in number, but one in kind. Their denial is the mark. Their doctrinal rebellion identifies them. Their refusal to confess the truth about Christ places them under the title antichrist.

How the Singular and the Plural Work Together

At this point the reader can see why John's language must be handled with care. He uses both singular and plural forms, and both are important. If one speaks only of a single antichrist, he ignores John's repeated insistence that many antichrists were already present. If one speaks only of many antichrists, he risks flattening John's expectation that antichrist was also "coming" in a recognized and climactic sense. Scripture itself requires a more refined understanding. The singular and the plural work together, not against each other.

The plural emphasizes multiplication, diffusion, and historical presence. Antichrist is not a solitary anomaly. It appears in numerous deceivers, teachers, defectors, and enemies of the truth. It spreads through many mouths, many systems, many denials, and many assaults on Christ's people. This explains why John can say "many antichrists have arisen." He is describing a phenomenon already visible across the churches. The danger had breadth. The church was facing not one isolated voice but a developing network of christological falsehood and spiritual deception.

The singular, however, emphasizes identity, quality, and concentrated recognition. John can speak of "the antichrist" because all the many antichrists share one common nature. They belong to the same rebellion. They express the same anti-Christ principle. They deny the same Lord in different forms. In that sense, "the antichrist" can function as a collective designation for the whole antichristic phenomenon, just as 2 John 7 speaks of many deceivers and then says, "this is the deceiver and the antichrist." The singular can also leave room for a climactic manifestation of the same hostility in more concentrated form, but John's own stress in these passages is not first on isolated individuality. It is on present doctrinal opposition and the common spiritual character binding all such deceivers together.

This is the point at which many prophetic treatments go wrong. They seize the singular and ignore the plural. John does the opposite. He mentions the anticipated coming of antichrist and then immediately directs attention to the many antichrists already present. The practical weight of his teaching falls upon recognition in the present. That must remain our starting point as well. Any model of antichrist that cannot account for first-century deceivers whom John himself identified is already defective. The doctrine must be broad enough to include John's historical reality and precise enough to preserve John's theological definition.

Why John's Language Must Control the Definition

Once John's own language is allowed to stand, the answer to the chapter's central question becomes clear. The Bible does not speak of antichrist as though there were only one future individual and nothing more. The biblical doctrine, as John gives it, includes an expected coming antichristic reality, but it also includes many present opponents already active in the apostolic age. Antichrist is therefore both singular and plural, both anticipated and already manifest, both doctrinal and historical. It arises especially through deceivers who deny the truth about Jesus Christ, depart from apostolic fellowship, and seek to draw others away from the truth.

For that reason, all later discussion in this book must remain under John's control. When later chapters consider apostasy, the man of lawlessness, persecuting rulers, beastly power, and the final organized order of rebellion, those discussions must not overwrite John's definition. The term *antichrist* belongs to John's letters, and John anchors it in doctrinal denial of the Son. That is the foundation. Other passages may illuminate the development, concentration, public manifestation, and final judgment of antichristic opposition, but they must not be used to erase the core truth John has already established. The church must begin where Scripture begins.

This also gives the believer a faithful method of discernment. The first question to ask is not, "Who controls world events?" or "What headline appears ominous?" The first question is, "What is being taught about Jesus Christ?" Does a teacher confess that Jesus is the Christ? Does he acknowledge the Father and the Son? Does he confess Jesus Christ as having come in the flesh? Does he remain in the apostolic message heard from the beginning? If not, John supplies the necessary category. The issue is not harmless deviation. It is antichristic rebellion. The church therefore guards itself by clinging to the truth of Christ, testing the spirits by the apostolic Word, and refusing every doctrine that strips the Son of His true glory.

In this way the doctrine of antichrist becomes immediately practical. It calls the church to doctrinal vigilance, spiritual sobriety, and covenant loyalty. It warns believers not to be impressed by mere religious language, institutional prestige, or claims of spiritual authority. It trains them to judge every message by the truth of Jesus Christ. It also reminds them that antichrist did not begin yesterday and does not wait passively for the end. It was already in the world in the first century, it was already troubling the churches, and it was already proving that the last hour had arrived in a decisive redemptive-historical sense. That is why John wrote as he did, and that is why the church must still hear him with seriousness.

The opening chapter of this book, then, must leave no uncertainty. Antichrist in Scripture is not limited to one simplistic future caricature. According to John, many antichrists had already arisen. Yet these many did not dissolve the category into vagueness, for John could still speak of "the antichrist" as the recognized and unified character of that rebellion. The church must therefore reject every reductionist theory that ignores either side of John's teaching. The proper biblical starting point is this: antichrist is the many-sided but recognizably unified opposition to Jesus Christ, especially in doctrinal denial, already present in the apostolic age and moving through history toward its fuller exposure under the sovereign judgment of God.

Chapter 2. The Antichrist Already at Work: Present Reality and Final Expectation

The Meaning of "Last Hour"

When John writes, "Young children, it is the last hour," he is not speaking carelessly, nor is He using empty religious language designed to stir emotion without content. He is making a decisive theological statement about the age in which the church was already living. The expression "last hour" in 1 John 2:18 places his readers in a time of culmination, exposure, and separation. The Messiah had already come. He had already lived, died, been raised, and ascended. The apostles had already proclaimed the gospel throughout the known world. The Christian congregation had already been established on the foundation of apostolic truth. Therefore, the appearance of deceivers in that period was not some strange interruption in Jehovah's purpose. It was one of the very signs that the church had entered the climactic stage of redemptive history. John does not treat antichrist as something disconnected from that era. He treats it as one of the marks that proved the church was already standing in the last-hour conflict between truth and falsehood.

That point must be grasped at the outset, because many readers assume the "last days" or the "last hour" are references only to a distant closing generation near Christ's return. Yet the apostles themselves speak as men already living in that decisive era. John does not say that a last hour would eventually come many centuries later. He says, "it is the last hour." His language is immediate and pastoral. He is interpreting current events in the light of God's revealed purpose. The churches were seeing defections, denials, counterfeit teaching, and rival claims about Jesus Christ. Those developments did not mean God had lost control. They meant that Christ's warning about coming deception was being fulfilled within the age of the church itself.

This understanding also prevents a serious distortion in prophetic interpretation. If the "last hour" is pushed entirely into the future, then antichrist becomes exclusively future as well. But John will not allow that. He expressly grounds his statement in what was already happening before his readers. "Even now many antichrists have arisen; from this we know that it is the last hour" (1 John 2:18). In other words, the presence of antichristic deception was not merely something to await; it was already evidence that the final age had dawned. The church was not simply looking toward a future crisis. It was already living within the conflict that would continue until Christ's return.

There is also a practical force in John's use of "last hour." It means that false doctrine concerning Christ is never a small matter. It is not a harmless academic dispute. It belongs to the final battle line between God's truth and satanic deception. John wants believers to understand the seriousness of doctrinal compromise. To depart from the truth about the Son is not simply to take a wrong turn in minor theology. It is to move into the sphere of antichrist. That is why the church must not treat the "last hour" as a phrase of mere chronology. It is a theological category describing an era of intensified spiritual conflict, doctrinal testing, and decisive allegiance.

The same perspective appears elsewhere in the New Testament. Paul tells Timothy that "in later times some will fall away from the faith, paying attention to deceitful spirits and teachings of demons" (1 Timothy 4:1). His point is not that such corruption belongs only to some unreachable future. It is that the Spirit had already spoken of a period in which demonic deception would invade the professing sphere. That aligns with John's own language. The apostolic church was not naïve about what lay ahead. It knew that the age after Christ's first coming would be marked not only by gospel proclamation, but also by counterfeit teaching, doctrinal revolt, and anti-Christ opposition from within and without.

The Spirit of Antichrist Already in the World

John makes the matter even plainer in 1 John 4:3: "every inspired expression that does not confess Jesus does not originate with God. Furthermore, this is the antichrist's inspired expression which you have heard was coming, and now it is already in the world." This statement is decisive for the whole doctrine. John does not merely say that antichrist will one day arrive. He says that the antichristic spirit, expression, or influence was already present in the world in his own day. That means the church must think of antichrist in two related ways. There is a coming and more public manifestation of antichristic rebellion, but there is also an already-present principle, energy, and expression of that rebellion active in history.

This "spirit of antichrist" language is especially important because it protects the reader from a shallow, overly narrow view. Antichrist is not first a newspaper identity to be guessed. It is a doctrinal and spiritual force opposing the truth of Jesus Christ. John places the emphasis on confession. Does a message confess the true Jesus? Does it align with the apostolic witness concerning the Son of God come in the flesh? Does it uphold the Father and the Son as Scripture reveals Them? If not, that message does not come from God, whatever outward attractiveness it may have. It belongs instead to the sphere of antichrist. John therefore trains the church to identify antichrist by theology before history, by doctrine before drama, and by confession before outward display.

This has enduring relevance because the church is often tempted to imagine antichrist only in gross or spectacular forms. John warns against that error. The spirit of antichrist can work through refined language, persuasive teaching, and religious claims that sound elevated while denying the truth about Jesus Christ. It does not need to announce itself bluntly. It can wear a Christian mask. It can speak in the vocabulary of faith while hollowing out the substance of faith. That is why John commands believers to test the spirits (1 John 4:1). Discernment is necessary precisely because falsehood often comes clothed in spiritual pretension.

Second John 7 confirms the same reality. "Many deceivers have gone out into the world, those not confessing Jesus Christ as coming in the flesh. This is the deceiver and the antichrist." Again, John combines plurality and unity. There are many deceivers, but their many voices share one antichristic character. Their denial of Jesus Christ is not a random intellectual mistake. It is part of a common hostility to the truth of God. They form a recognizable class because they all attack the same center: the person and saving revelation of Christ.

This means the church must resist the temptation to treat antichrist only as a late-stage public phenomenon. The antichristic spirit is already active whenever Christ is denied, reduced, redefined, or replaced. John's concern is not speculative chronology. His concern is present fidelity. The church must know that the danger is immediate. A congregation may be harmed by antichristic influence long before any final concentration of evil appears on the stage of history. Every denial of the Son, every refusal of the incarnation, every attack on the Father-Son relationship, every substitute christology, and every corrupt spiritual message that departs from apostolic truth belongs in this category.

It is also worth observing that John says this antichristic influence is "already in the world." The world, in Johannine thought, is the organized human order in rebellion against God. It is the realm of darkness, unbelief, hatred of truth, and opposition to the Son. Therefore, antichrist is not an accidental feature in the world. It belongs organically to a world-system that rejects divine revelation. This is why the church should not be surprised that false teaching about Christ arises again and again in history. The world does not receive the truth gladly. It produces alternatives, distortions, and denials because it does not want the true Christ to reign over it.

Why the Apostolic Age Already Experienced Antichrist

The apostolic age was not merely the age of pure proclamation; it was also the age in which falsehood began to press itself openly against the apostolic message. John's insistence that many antichrists had already arisen means that the conflict was not delayed until the church lost its first-century setting. On the contrary, while apostles were still living, deceivers were already spreading. This should sober anyone who imagines that proximity to sacred history automatically protects the church from corruption. John's churches had apostolic teaching, yet they still had to contend with antichrists. That is why every generation of Christians must remain vigilant. External nearness to the things of God does not guarantee loyalty to the truth of God.

The immediate context of 1 John 2 shows that the antichrists of John's day were not merely hostile outsiders. "They went out from us, but they were not of us" (1 John 2:19). John is describing secessionists, defectors, and deceivers who had emerged from within the professing sphere. Their departure revealed their lack of genuine identity with apostolic truth. This is one reason the apostolic age already experienced antichrist so clearly. The conflict was not only between the church and paganism. It was also between apostolic Christianity and false claimants who wished to redefine Christ while still moving in relation to the Christian community.

This pattern had already been foreseen. Jesus warned in Matthew 24:23–25 that false christs and false prophets would arise and would attempt to mislead. He told His disciples beforehand so that they would not be overtaken by surprise. The church was not left without warning. Christ prepared His followers to expect deception, counterfeit claims, and manipulative displays. Therefore, when John later says that many antichrists had arisen, he is not announcing a failure of prophecy but its fulfillment. The Lord had spoken. The apostles had repeated the warning. The church was now seeing the reality.

Acts 20:29–30 shows the same expectation from another angle. Paul warns the Ephesian elders that savage wolves will come in among the flock and that men from among their own number will arise, speaking twisted things in order to draw away disciples after them. This is profoundly significant. The antichristic threat in the apostolic age was not merely philosophical opposition from the outside. It was also ecclesial corruption, doctrinal distortion, and factional drawing away from within. This is why John does not present antichrist as only a distant climax. He speaks of many antichrists in the present because the apostolic churches were already contending with those who denied the truth and sought to gather followers after themselves.

The first-century setting therefore proves a critical point for the whole doctrine of antichrist: the church must never think that antichrist belongs only to a final generation while being absent from all previous history. John himself denies that by his plain language. Antichrist was already at work while the apostolic witness was still being delivered. That fact protects the reader from two opposite errors. On one side, it protects against the sensational claim that antichrist can only be a single future person. On the other side, it protects against the flattening idea that there is no final concentration or culmination of antichristic rebellion at all. The apostolic age gives us the seed form already active, thereby preparing the church to understand both continuity and escalation.

This also reveals why the church's greatest need is not speculation but doctrinal stability. John's answer to the presence of antichrist is not panic. It is abiding in what was heard from the beginning (1 John 2:24). The believer is protected not by fascination with prophetic fear, but by loyalty to apostolic truth. The church must remain in the teaching concerning the Son. It must test the spirits. It must reject deceivers. It must hold fast to the confession of Jesus Christ. That was true in the first century, and it remains true now.

Present Operation and Future Intensification

The biblical data compel a balanced doctrine. Antichrist is already present in principle, operation, and manifestation, yet Scripture also teaches a future intensification and fuller unveiling of lawless rebellion. John provides the "already," while other passages help the reader understand the "not yet" dimension of final concentration. Both truths must be maintained if the church is to avoid confusion.

John's letters establish beyond dispute that antichrist was already operative in the apostolic era. The spirit of antichrist was already in the world. Many antichrists had already arisen. Many deceivers had already gone out into the world. That is the present reality. Yet John also says, "you have heard that antichrist is coming" (1 John 2:18). His language leaves room for expectation beyond the immediate manifestations already troubling the churches. He does not treat the matter as exhausted simply because many antichrists had appeared. Instead, he teaches that the present outbreak confirms the seriousness of the age and prepares the church to think soberly about what will come.

Here a brief appeal to 2 Thessalonians 2:3–12 is useful, though the larger treatment belongs later in the book. Paul speaks there of a coming apostasy and of "the man of lawlessness," whose revelation is associated with deception, false signs, and open self-exaltation. That passage should not be forced into John's language as though the terms were interchangeable in a simplistic way. John must define antichrist, and Paul must define the man of lawlessness. Yet the two passages clearly stand in harmony as witnesses to a broad biblical pattern: what is already at work in seed and spirit reaches a more open and concentrated manifestation in history. Paul even says that "the mystery of lawlessness is already at work" (2 Thessalonians 2:7). That wording closely parallels John's doctrine of present antichristic activity. The rebellion is active before its fullest exposure. The corruption operates before its final unveiling.

Matthew 24:23–25 contributes to the same picture. Jesus speaks not merely of isolated errors but of intensified deception capable of misleading many. False christs and false prophets arise with persuasive force. The warning is not casual. It assumes a conflict that can deepen and spread. In that sense, the antichristic phenomenon is both already and increasingly. It is present in every era where Christ is denied, but it moves toward fuller maturity as rebellion against God hardens and organizes itself more openly against His Son.

This pattern of present operation and future intensification is entirely consistent with how Scripture often describes evil. Sin was already in the world long before it ripened in particular judgments. False prophets were already active before great acts of apostasy became visible. The mystery of lawlessness was already at work before the lawless one was fully revealed. Likewise, the spirit of antichrist was already in the world before the church had seen the full historical concentration of anti-Christ power. The believer should therefore expect continuity and climax. The roots are already present; the mature expression comes later. The current is already running; the flood may yet swell.

This understanding also helps preserve sobriety in interpretation. A Christian does not need to claim that every deceiver is the final climactic expression of antichrist in order to recognize that he is truly antichristic. John already gives the category for present use. Nor must the Christian deny the possibility of a fuller future concentration in order to honor John's teaching about present reality. Scripture itself requires a doctrine large enough to include both. There are many antichrists, and there is antichrist coming. The spirit is already active, and the final exposure still lies ahead. The church must hold both truths without collapsing one into the other.

Why Christians Must Reject Date-Setting Sensationalism

Because Scripture teaches both present activity and future expectation, believers are often tempted to move beyond biblical clarity into sensationalism. This temptation has done great damage. Again and again, readers of prophecy have attached the label antichrist to particular personalities, dates, institutions, inventions, or political fears with a level of certainty that Scripture itself does not authorize.

John's teaching acts as a strong corrective to such recklessness. His purpose is not to encourage feverish guessing. His purpose is to cultivate theological discernment and covenant faithfulness.

The first reason Christians must reject date-setting sensationalism is that John himself directs attention first to present doctrinal reality, not speculative chronology. He does not say, "Calculate the time and identify the final individual immediately." He says that many antichrists have already arisen and that the spirit of antichrist is already in the world. The danger, therefore, is not postponed until some future calendar point. It is a present spiritual threat requiring present vigilance. Date-setting often distracts the church from that urgent responsibility. It trains believers to stare outward at predicted timetables while neglecting the false teaching already working in their midst.

The second reason is that sensationalism often ignores the moral and theological purpose of prophecy. Jesus warned His disciples beforehand so that they would not be misled (Matthew 24:25). The goal of prophecy is steadfastness, not excitement. It is obedience, not panic. It is watchfulness joined to truth, not speculation joined to fear. Whenever prophetic study produces endless excitement over rumors, personalities, and alleged hidden fulfillments while neglecting holiness, doctrinal fidelity, and endurance, the purpose of Scripture has been distorted. John writes to anchor believers in the Son and in the apostolic message, not to turn them into anxious interpreters of every passing development.

The third reason is that date-setting tends to force the biblical data into artificial precision. Scripture certainly reveals enough for the church to know that evil will intensify, deception will increase, and Christ will triumph openly in the end. But it does not authorize every proposed timeline or every dogmatic identification advanced by speculative interpreters. John's own formulation is wiser. He teaches the church to recognize the antichristic principle already active while leaving room for the coming concentration of that rebellion. That approach is sober, biblical, and pastorally useful. It keeps the church alert without becoming unstable.

There is also a spiritual danger in repeated sensationalism: it dulls discernment. When believers are constantly told that this date, that event, or this public figure is certainly the final fulfillment, and then those claims collapse, confidence in biblical prophecy can be weakened. Worse, the church may become so fascinated with external predictions that it ceases to test teaching about Christ carefully. John would have the opposite outcome. He wants believers to know that antichrist is real, already active, and doctrinally identifiable. He wants them to discern falsehood by apostolic truth. That kind of vigilance does not rise and fall with every cultural panic.

A biblically grounded doctrine of antichrist, therefore, is neither dismissive nor sensational. It does not deny future intensification, and it does not postpone antichrist entirely to the end. It recognizes that the church has lived from the apostolic age onward in the presence of antichristic deception. It acknowledges that what is already present may yet reach a more open and climactic expression. And it keeps believers anchored not in prophetic theater, but in the confession of Jesus Christ, the Son of God, who came in the flesh and whom the Father sent for the salvation of His people.

For that reason, the church's task in every age is clear. It must listen carefully to John's warning. It must remember that the "last hour" had already begun in the apostolic era. It must recognize that the spirit of antichrist was already in the world when the New Testament itself was being written. It must understand that present deception and future intensification belong together in the biblical witness. And it must reject every approach that substitutes speculative excitement for doctrinal steadiness. The church does not overcome antichrist by guessing dates. It overcomes antichrist by abiding in the truth concerning Christ, testing every spirit by the apostolic Word, and refusing all teaching that denies the Son. In that way John's doctrine remains as urgent now as when he first wrote it, because antichrist is not merely a future possibility. It is a present reality moving through history toward its appointed exposure under the sovereign rule of Jehovah and the victorious appearing of His Son.

Chapter 3. The Doctrinal Lie of Antichrist: Denying the Christ, the Son, and the Incarnation

Denying That Jesus Is the Christ

The heart of the biblical doctrine of antichrist is not first political aggression, social upheaval, or visible tyranny. It is doctrinal rebellion centered on the person and identity of Jesus Christ. John states the matter with unmistakable clarity in 1 John 2:22: "Who is the liar if it is not the one that denies that Jesus is the Christ?" He then adds, "This is the antichrist." That definition is decisive. Antichrist is not merely someone who behaves badly, opposes religion in a vague sense, or promotes general wickedness. Antichrist is identified by a specific theological falsehood: the denial that Jesus is the Christ, the Messiah, the Anointed One sent by the Father. The first great lie of antichrist, therefore, is not simply that truth does not matter. It is that Jesus is not the One Scripture declares Him to be.

This is why the church must treat christological error as central rather than secondary. The title "Christ" is not an optional label. It identifies Jesus as the promised Messiah foretold in the Law, the Prophets, and the Writings. To deny that Jesus is the Christ is to reject the fulfillment of Jehovah's redemptive purpose. It is to say, in effect, that the promises of God do not reach their goal in Jesus of Nazareth. It is to sever the New Testament from the Old Testament, the fulfillment from the promise, and the gospel from the covenant purpose of God. John will not allow such denial to be softened into a respectable disagreement. He calls it a lie, and He calls the one who teaches it antichrist.

John 20:30–31 makes this point especially clear. John explains the purpose of his Gospel by saying that the signs of Jesus were recorded so "that you may believe that Jesus is the Christ, the Son of God, and that by believing you may have life in His name." The confession that Jesus is the Christ is therefore bound up with salvation itself. It is not a marginal doctrinal refinement reserved for specialists. It is part of the very truth by which life is received. If that is so, then denial of Jesus as the Christ is not a minor defect in theological vocabulary. It is an assault on the saving message of the gospel. The church cannot preserve the gospel while tolerating systematic rejection of Jesus' messianic identity.

This denial may take more than one form. Some deny Jesus by rejecting Him outright as the promised Messiah. Others claim to honor Him while redefining what Messiah means, stripping Him of His divine authority, His unique sonship, His redemptive mission, or His role as the sole way to the Father. Still others treat Him as merely one spiritual teacher among many, one religious example among others, or one stage in an evolving human consciousness. All such positions are antichristic in principle because they refuse the apostolic confession of who Jesus truly is. John does not leave room for halfway christologies. Either Jesus is the Christ in the biblical sense, or the teaching that denies Him belongs to the lie.

IDENTIFYING THE ANTICHRIST

The language of 1 John 2:22 also reminds the reader that false doctrine is moral as well as intellectual. John does not ask merely, "Who is mistaken?" He asks, "Who is the liar?" That is strong language, but it is fitting. The denial of Jesus as the Christ is not innocent. It is a revolt against the truth God has made known. It rejects the witness the Father has given concerning His Son. It contradicts the apostolic testimony established through the ministry, death, resurrection, and exaltation of Jesus Christ. Because this denial opposes divine revelation itself, John calls it what it is: a lie. Antichrist, then, is not defined first by institutional power but by doctrinal falsehood set against the revealed identity of Christ.

This is why every faithful treatment of antichrist must begin here. The church will go astray if it seeks antichrist only in dramatic future events while neglecting present denials of Jesus' true identity. Wherever the truth concerning Jesus as the Christ is opposed, reduced, or replaced, the lie of antichrist is already active. The first battlefield is doctrinal. The first line of defense is fidelity to the biblical confession that Jesus is the promised Messiah, the One anointed and sent by the Father, and the only Savior appointed for sinful mankind.

Denying the Father and the Son

John does not stop with the denial that Jesus is the Christ. He immediately deepens the matter by declaring that antichrist is "the one that denies the Father and the Son" (1 John 2:22). This statement shows that antichristic doctrine is not merely wrong about one figure in isolation. It is wrong about the relationship at the center of divine revelation. The Father has made Himself known through the Son, and the Son has come from the Father in perfect unity of purpose, nature, and testimony. To deny the Son is therefore to deny the Father as well. John makes this explicit in 1 John 2:23: "Everyone denying the Son does not have the Father either. He that confesses the Son has the Father also."

This is one of the most decisive statements in all of Scripture against the idea that a person may reject the true identity of Jesus and still remain in a valid relationship with God. John gives no room for such a claim. One cannot dismiss or redefine the Son and still claim to know the Father rightly. The Father and the Son cannot be separated without destroying the truth about both. Since the Father Himself has testified concerning the Son, any doctrine that rejects the Son is also a rejection of the Father's own witness.

The Gospel of John provides powerful support for this truth. In John 5:22–23, Jesus teaches that the Father has entrusted judgment to the Son "so that all may honor the Son just as they honor the Father." He adds that the one who does not honor the Son does not honor the Father who sent Him. That is decisive. The honor of the Father and the honor of the Son stand together. A teaching that claims reverence for God while withholding due honor from the Son is exposed by Jesus' own words as false. It is not a lesser form of devotion. It is a denial of the very One whom the Father has sent and exalted.

John 10:30–38 also bears directly on this issue. Jesus says, "I and the Father are one," and He identifies Himself as the One whom the Father sanctified and sent into the world. When He is accused of blasphemy, He does not retreat from His claim. Instead, He directs attention to the works that testify that "the Father is in Me, and I am in the Father." The passage does not dissolve the distinction between the Father and the Son, but it does establish a unity so profound that rejection of the Son becomes rejection of the Father's own self-disclosure. Antichristic doctrine therefore does more than misstate one article of theology. It attacks the revealed relationship through which God has made Himself known.

Luke 9:35 confirms the same reality from the Father's own declaration at the transfiguration: "This is My Son, the One chosen; listen to Him." The Father publicly identifies Jesus as His Son and commands men to hear Him. Any voice that refuses that command, diminishes that Sonship, or substitutes another christology stands directly against the Father's own testimony. It is not merely offering an alternate interpretation. It is rebelling against heaven's declaration.

This is why John's language is so uncompromising. The church often feels pressure to soften doctrinal lines in the name of outward harmony. Yet John insists that the truth about the Father and the Son is a line that must not be blurred. To deny the Son is not to choose another Christian emphasis. It is to abandon the living center of revelation. The Father has spoken through His Son. The Father has sent His Son. The Father has borne witness concerning His Son. Therefore, any teaching that refuses the Son or corrupts His identity is antichristic by definition.

The implications are immense. The church must never evaluate doctrines concerning Jesus as though they were detachable from one's view of God. A false christology always carries with it a false theology. If the Son is denied, the Father is denied. If the Son is redefined, the Father's revelation is distorted. If the Son is displaced, the Father's purpose is opposed. John's doctrine exposes the seriousness of the matter. Antichrist is not simply anti-Jesus in a narrow sense. It is anti-Father-and-Son. It opposes God as He has made Himself known in the sending of His Son into the world.

Not Confessing Jesus Christ as Having Come in the Flesh

John gives a further doctrinal test in 1 John 4:2–3 and 2 John 7. Every inspired expression that confesses Jesus Christ as having come in the flesh is from God, but every inspired expression that does not confess Jesus is not from God. In 2 John 7, he writes, "Many deceivers have gone out into the world, those not confessing Jesus Christ as coming in the flesh. This is the deceiver and the antichrist." Here the lie of antichrist is directed specifically against the incarnation. The issue is not simply whether Jesus existed, nor merely whether He was a teacher of unusual influence. The issue is whether He truly came in the flesh as the Christ.

This confession is essential because it safeguards the reality of the incarnation against every spiritualized distortion. John 1:1 declares that "the Word was with God, and the Word was God," and John 1:14 adds, "the Word became flesh and dwelt among us." These two truths must be held together. The eternal Word did not cease to be who He was, but He truly became flesh. He entered human history in real humanity. He was not an illusion, a passing appearance, or a symbolic projection. He came bodily into the world as the promised Christ. John insists on this because any denial of the incarnation empties the gospel of its saving substance.

If Jesus did not truly come in the flesh, then the gospel accounts are broken at their center. His obedience would not be genuine human obedience. His suffering would not be real suffering. His death would not be an actual sacrificial death borne in human nature. His resurrection would not be bodily triumph over death. The atoning work of Christ requires the truth that the Son truly came in the flesh. Antichristic doctrine strikes here because it seeks to dissolve the saving reality of what God has done in Christ. A christology detached from the incarnation cannot save because it no longer has the biblical Christ.

This also explains why John links false prophets and deceivers with this denial. The incarnation is not a peripheral doctrine that can be adjusted without consequence. It is part of the foundation of the faith. Those who reject it are not merely offering a variant Christian emphasis. They are replacing the apostolic Christ with another figure. John's language is intentionally severe because the danger is severe. The church must learn from Him that false spirituality often appears most pious when it has become most detached from the flesh-and-blood reality of God's saving work in His Son.

To confess that Jesus Christ has come in the flesh also guards the church from every attempt to divide the historical Jesus from the divine Christ in a way that destroys their unity. John will not permit a separation between "Jesus" and "Christ" as though the latter were only a temporary spiritual force resting upon the former. He speaks of "Jesus Christ as coming in the flesh." The One who came in the flesh is Jesus Christ. The historical Jesus and the Messiah are one and the same. The Son did not merely visit a human shell or temporarily use a human instrument. He Himself came in the flesh. That truth stands at the core of the apostolic confession.

Because the incarnation lies so close to the center of the gospel, denial of it becomes one of the clearest identifying marks of antichrist. The church must therefore test every teaching by this question: Does it confess the biblical Christ who truly came in the flesh? Does it uphold the full reality of His incarnation? Does it preserve the unity of His person and the truth of His saving mission? If not, however sophisticated the language may be, it stands under John's verdict. It is the deceiver and the antichrist.

Why Christological Error Is Not Secondary

One of the most destructive habits in theological compromise is the tendency to treat error about Christ as though it were merely a difference in emphasis. John's letters destroy that illusion. For John, christological error is not secondary because Christ is not secondary. The truth about Jesus Christ stands at the center of revelation, salvation, worship, and eternal life. If the church loses clarity here, it does not simply lose a refined point of doctrine. It loses the truth that gives life.

This is why John writes with sharp contrasts. Truth and lie. Confession and denial. God and not God. The Father and the Son, or neither. Such language may appear severe to a generation that prefers blurred edges, but it is the severity of divine truth confronting mortal error. John knows that eternal issues are at stake. To deny Jesus as the Christ, to deny the Son, or to refuse His coming in the flesh is to move outside the apostolic faith. That is why the church must never apologize for insisting upon sound doctrine concerning Christ. Such insistence is not harshness. It is fidelity.

John 20:31 shows again why this cannot be secondary: belief that Jesus is the Christ, the Son of God, is bound up with life in His name. The church does not preach Christ merely to complete its doctrinal system. It preaches Christ because He is the object of saving faith. If men are directed to a false christ, they are not merely intellectually misinformed; they are spiritually ruined unless they repent and believe the truth. That is why the apostles guarded the identity of Jesus with such seriousness. They understood that salvation itself was bound to the true confession of the Son.

There is also a worship dimension to this issue. John 5:23 teaches that all are to honor the Son just as they honor the Father. False doctrine about Christ inevitably corrupts worship. If the Son is diminished, honor is withheld. If His identity is twisted, devotion is misdirected. If His incarnation is denied, gratitude for His saving work is emptied of its biblical content. Christological error therefore does not stay in the classroom. It enters the sanctuary. It changes prayer, praise, proclamation, obedience, and the hope of eternal life.

For that reason, the church must never be ashamed to draw doctrinal boundaries around the person of Christ. Those boundaries are not man-made barriers erected to preserve sectarian pride. They are scriptural necessities arising from the truth God has revealed. The apostles did not say, "As long as people speak positively about Jesus, the details are unimportant." They said the opposite. They tested confession. They warned against deceivers. They identified denials. They called certain teachings antichristic. That apostolic pattern remains binding. A church that ceases to guard the doctrine of Christ has ceased to guard the gospel.

This also means that Christians must develop discernment deeper than slogans. Many false teachings use biblical language while smuggling in another meaning. They may speak of Jesus, the Son, the Christ, the Spirit, salvation, and God, yet attach definitions foreign to Scripture. John's test reaches beneath vocabulary to substance. What Jesus is being confessed? Is He the Christ promised in Scripture? Is He the Son whom the Father sent? Has He truly come in the flesh? Does the teaching preserve the Father-Son relationship as Scripture presents it? These are not abstract questions. They are the very means by which the church distinguishes truth from antichristic falsehood.

Theological Treason Against the Gospel

When all of John's statements are taken together, the lie of antichrist must be understood as theological treason against the gospel itself. It is treason because it turns against the truth once delivered. It is theological because its primary battlefield is doctrine. And it is against the gospel because the gospel stands or falls with the true identity of Jesus Christ. To deny the Christ, the Son, and the incarnation is not to quarrel with one piece of Christian thought. It is to strike at the living center of the Christian message.

The gospel announces what God has done in His Son. The Father sent the Son into the world. The Son came in the flesh. Jesus is the

Christ. Eternal life is found in Him. The one who has the Son has life. The one who does not have the Son of God does not have life. Therefore, when antichrist denies the Son, it does more than challenge a doctrine; it opposes the way of salvation God has made known. It seeks to leave sinners with a name of Christ emptied of Christ's truth.

This is why John does not treat the deceivers as harmless voices in a broad spiritual conversation. In 2 John 7 he calls them "many deceivers." In 1 John 2:22 he calls the denier "the liar." In 1 John 4:3 he says their teaching is not from God. Such language is necessary because the lie is destructive. A false christ cannot save. A denied Son cannot mediate. An unincarnate redeemer cannot die for sin in the biblical sense. A confession emptied of the truth is no confession at all. Antichrist, therefore, is not simply a competitor among doctrines. It is a rebellion against the only gospel by which sinners are rescued.

The church must learn from this that fidelity to Christology is an act of loyalty to God Himself. To confess the Son truly is to receive the Father's testimony. To honor the Son is to honor the Father who sent Him. To confess Jesus Christ as having come in the flesh is to stand within the apostolic witness. To remain in that confession is to remain in the truth. This is why theological precision about Christ is not cold or sterile. It is worshipful, necessary, and life-giving. The believer clings to the truth about Christ because there is no life apart from Him as He truly is.

The doctrinal lie of antichrist will continue to appear in many forms. It may be bold or subtle, scholarly or popular, ancient or modern, hostile or seemingly reverent. But its essence remains the same. It denies that Jesus is the Christ. It denies the Father and the Son. It refuses to confess Jesus Christ as having come in the flesh. Wherever these denials appear, John has already given the church the right name for them. They belong to antichrist. And wherever the church holds fast the apostolic confession, honoring the Son as the Father commands and proclaiming the incarnate Christ as the only Savior, the lie is exposed and the truth stands firm.

Chapter 4. Antichrist From Within: Apostasy, Deception, and Hatred of the Faithful

"They Went Out From Us"

One of the most sobering truths in the Johannine doctrine of antichrist is that antichrist does not appear only as an obvious outside enemy. John writes in 1 John 2:19, "They went out from us, but they were not of us; for if they had been of us, they would have remained with us. But they went out, that it might become plain that they all are not of us." Those words immediately correct a shallow understanding of spiritual danger. John does not describe antichrist merely as pagan hostility from beyond the congregation. He describes persons who had once moved within the visible sphere of the Christian community and then departed from apostolic truth. Their withdrawal was not simply a change of preference, temperament, or religious style. It was a disclosure of what they truly were. Their departure exposed a deeper reality: they did not belong to the apostolic fellowship in the sense that mattered most.

This passage must be handled carefully. John is not saying that everyone who physically leaves one local congregation is automatically antichrist. His point is much more serious and much more specific. He is speaking of those who separate from apostolic truth, who reject the confession of Christ, and who break from the fellowship built upon the truth the apostles received from the Lord Jesus Christ. The issue is doctrinal and spiritual defection. They were outwardly associated with the people of God, but they did not remain in the truth that marks the people of God. John's language shows that antichrist often emerges where outward profession once existed. That is what makes the danger so grave. The threat does not always come wearing the clothing of an obvious enemy. It may arise through persons once counted among the visible company of believers.

This is why the church must never judge spiritual safety by proximity alone. A person may be near the congregation, near Christian language, near biblical discussion, and near sacred things, yet still harbor rebellion against the truth of Christ. Judas Iscariot lived in the closest outward proximity to the Lord Jesus and yet was not loyal to Him. John's words in 1 John 2:19 show the same principle working in the church after the ascension of Christ. The visible company can contain those who later reveal that their hearts were never surrendered to the truth they professed with their lips. When they depart, oppose, corrupt, and deny, their departure is not merely organizational. It is revelatory. It uncovers the fact that their connection was external rather than spiritual and doctrinal.

John's statement also explains why antichrist from within is so dangerous. External enemies are often easier to identify because they declare their opposition openly. Internal deceivers can work quietly for a time. They may speak the church's language while hollowing out its meaning. They may claim devotion to Christ while introducing a different christology. They may use the vocabulary of Scripture while steadily moving away from the substance of apostolic truth. Only in time does their true direction become unmistakable. John therefore teaches the church not to be naïve. Not every association with the people of God is genuine fellowship in the truth of God. Antichrist can stand near the congregation before it finally goes out from the congregation.

Apostasy as Defection From Apostolic Truth

The departure John describes is not a bare social separation. It is apostasy, that is, defection from the apostolic faith. Apostasy must not be reduced to mere institutional change or disagreement over secondary matters. In the context of John's letters and the broader New Testament witness, apostasy is a turning away from the truth God has revealed in His Son. It is rebellion against the message heard from the beginning. It is refusal to continue in the doctrine of Christ. That is why 2 John 9 states, "Everyone who pushes ahead and does not remain in the teaching of the Christ does not have God. He that remains in this teaching is the one that has both the Father and the Son." The apostate does not merely step into a different interpretive school. He moves outside the teaching that gives access to the Father and the Son.

This is why the language of "progress" is often spiritually deceptive. John warns about the one who "pushes ahead" and does not remain in the teaching of the Christ. That warning remains painfully relevant. False teachers often present themselves as spiritually advanced, intellectually refined, or liberated from what they portray as narrow older understandings. Yet John says that if their movement carries them beyond the teaching of Christ, they do not have God. That is not advancement. It is abandonment. Apostasy frequently advertises itself as deeper wisdom while in truth it is departure from the faith once delivered. The Christian congregation must never confuse novelty with maturity. The standard is not whether a teaching sounds fresh, bold, or sophisticated. The standard is whether it remains in the doctrine of Christ.

The same pattern appears in 1 Timothy 4:1–3, where Paul says that "in later times some will fall away from the faith, paying attention to deceitful spirits and teachings of demons." Though the fuller Pauline treatment belongs later in this book, the verse is highly relevant here because it confirms the apostolic pattern already seen in John. Defection arises in the professing sphere. It is not only outward opposition from unbelieving society. It is a falling away from within, driven by spiritual deception and false doctrine. The church must therefore understand apostasy not merely as moral decline, though moral corruption often accompanies it, but as surrender to teachings that depart from the truth.

Second Timothy 3:1–5 also sheds light on the moral shape of apostasy. Paul describes men who are lovers of self, lovers of money, boastful, arrogant, slanderous, without self-control, brutal, treacherous, swollen with conceit, lovers of pleasures rather than lovers of God, "holding to a form of godliness, although they have denied its power." That last phrase is especially significant. The apostate does not always discard religious appearance. He may preserve a form of godliness while rejecting its living power. Outward structure can remain while inward truth is lost. This is one reason antichrist from within is so perilous. It often wears a religious face. It may appear disciplined, organized, persuasive, and devout. Yet its center is hollow because it does not remain in the truth of Christ.

Apostasy, then, is not simply going away from a group. It is going away from revealed truth. It is a doctrinal and spiritual rebellion that breaks from apostolic teaching while often retaining enough religious form to mislead the unwary. This is why John's warning must remain fixed in the church's mind. The issue is not merely who once stood among us. The issue is who remains in the teaching of Christ. Persistence in apostolic truth marks genuine fellowship. Departure from that truth reveals the antichristic character of the defection.

False Teachers as Antichristic Agents

John commands, "Beloved ones, do not believe every inspired expression, but examine the inspired expressions to see whether they originate with God, because many false prophets have gone out into the world" (1 John 4:1). This command joins directly to the subject of antichrist because false teachers are one of the primary instruments through which antichristic deception spreads. Antichrist is not merely a vague hostile atmosphere. It speaks. It teaches. It persuades. It advances its rebellion through messages, doctrines, and messengers that seek to detach people from the truth of Christ. The battlefield is therefore doctrinal before it becomes openly institutional or political. False teachers function as active agents of antichrist because they carry and distribute the lie.

Acts 20:29–30 gives this warning in unforgettable terms. Paul tells the Ephesian elders, "I know that after my departure fierce wolves will enter in among you, not sparing the flock; and from among your own selves men will arise and speak twisted things, to draw away the disciples after them." This description harmonizes perfectly with John's concern. The false teachers are not harmless eccentrics. They are wolves. They do not nourish the flock; they devour it. They do not clarify the truth; they twist it. They do not direct attention to Christ alone; they draw disciples after themselves. Self-exaltation, distortion of truth, and injury to the congregation belong to their character. In that sense, antichristic teaching is always predatory. It uses the language of spirituality to consume, scatter, and enslave.

Second Peter 2:1–3 strengthens this picture by declaring that false teachers will arise "among you," secretly introducing destructive heresies, even denying the Master who bought them, bringing swift destruction upon themselves. Peter's emphasis on secrecy is essential. False teaching often enters covertly. It seldom announces itself as poison. It arrives quietly, clothed in persuasive words, appealing personalities, and selective use of Scripture. This is why the church must remain doctrinally watchful. False teachers do not need open hostility in order to do immense damage. Quiet corruption is often more deadly than loud opposition because it can spread while many are still calling it harmless.

Peter goes on in 2 Peter 2:15–22 to show that false teachers are marked not only by doctrinal corruption but also by moral crookedness. They have forsaken the straight path. They entice unstable souls. They promise freedom while they themselves are slaves of corruption. Their teaching is not detached from their character. False doctrine and moral disorder grow together because both arise from rebellion against God's truth. Jude says the same in verses 3 and 4, urging believers to contend earnestly for the faith once for all handed down to the holy ones, because certain men have slipped in unnoticed, ungodly persons who turn the grace of God into sensuality and deny our only Master and Lord, Jesus Christ. Again the pattern is internal infiltration, doctrinal corruption, and moral revolt.

Jude 8–13 then draws the portrait with even darker colors. These men reject authority, revile glorious ones, are selfish shepherds feeding themselves, waterless clouds, fruitless trees, wild waves of the sea, and wandering stars for whom the blackness of darkness has been reserved. Such imagery shows that false teachers are not merely mistaken thinkers. They are destructive forces within the visible sphere of religion. They feed on the flock instead of feeding it. They promise refreshment but give none. They possess outward motion and noise, yet no life-giving substance. These are antichristic agents because they oppose the truth of Christ while operating in the realm of profession.

John's warning in 2 John 9–11 therefore becomes all the more necessary. Whoever does not remain in the teaching of Christ does not have God, and the believer must not receive such a one into his house or give him a greeting that blesses his evil work. John is not forbidding common civility. He is forbidding spiritual partnership with deceivers. The church must not become an open platform for those who undermine the doctrine of Christ. Hospitality becomes wicked when it functions as endorsement of falsehood. Here again the church sees that antichrist works through real teachers and real ministries. Discernment is therefore not optional. It is a moral duty.

Why Antichrist Hates Christ's True Followers

Antichrist from within is not content merely to alter doctrine. It also develops hatred toward those who remain faithful to Christ. This hatred may show itself in slander, exclusion, intimidation, mockery, pressure, and organized opposition. Jesus prepared His disciples for this reality in John 15:18–21: "If the world hates you, you know that it has hated me before it hated you. If you were part of the world, the world would be fond of what is its own. Now because you are no part of the world, but I have chosen you out of the world, on this account the world hates you." Though Jesus is speaking of the world broadly, His words apply with particular force to antichristic hostility because antichrist belongs to the world's rebellion against the Son. What the world hates in Christ it will also hate in those who belong to Christ.

This hatred is not irrational when viewed from the standpoint of spiritual warfare. The faithful Christian, by remaining in apostolic truth, exposes the lie. A congregation that holds fast to the doctrine of Christ stands as a rebuke to false teachers. Truth unmasks deception simply by being truth. For that reason, antichristic agents do not remain neutral toward those who refuse their teaching. They resent them. They seek to marginalize them. They portray fidelity as harshness, obedience as rigidity, and separation from falsehood as unloving conduct. In this way hatred often disguises itself as moral superiority. The faithful are condemned not because they have done evil, but because they refuse to join the rebellion.

The letters of John themselves reflect this conflict. The deceivers had not merely developed private opinions. They had broken fellowship. They had gone out. They had created a line of division around falsehood. Those who remained loyal to apostolic teaching necessarily stood against them. Whenever that occurs, animosity follows. The faithful become inconvenient. Their continued confession of the Son, the Father, and the incarnation stands as a witness against apostate teaching. Thus antichrist's hatred is deeply theological. It is hatred of Christ reflected onto Christ's people.

This same pattern can be seen in the broader apostolic witness. False teachers seek disciples after themselves, not after Christ alone. Anyone who resists their distortions becomes an obstacle to their ambition. That is why their hostility often intensifies when their teaching is challenged by Scripture. They may claim to be broad-minded, gracious, or spiritually mature, but when the doctrine of Christ is defended against them, their true posture appears. Jude's language about grumblers, malcontents, boasters, and flatterers reveals that false teachers are often driven by self-interest as much as by doctrinal corruption. Their opposition to the faithful grows from a deeper root of pride.

The church must therefore not be surprised when loyalty to Christ draws organized resistance, even from within the professing sphere. Jesus already said, "a slave is not greater than his master. If they have persecuted me, they will persecute you also" (John 15:20). That principle includes not only pagan persecution but also antichristic opposition arising in religious settings. The Lord was rejected by many who claimed to honor God. His followers should expect similar treatment from those who claim spiritual authority while denying the truth of the Son. Hatred of the faithful is one of the fruits of antichristic rebellion because antichrist cannot tolerate enduring witness to the real Christ.

The Moral and Ecclesial Shape of Antichrist

When the passages in John, Acts, Paul, Peter, and Jude are brought together, a clear picture emerges of the moral and ecclesial shape of antichrist. It is moral because antichrist is never merely a matter of abstract ideas. It involves pride, rebellion, deception, sensuality, greed, self-love, and hatred of the truth. It is ecclesial because it operates in relation to the visible people of God. It seeks entrance, influence, followers, and legitimacy within the sphere of religion. Antichrist from within is therefore not only false doctrine in the abstract. It is false doctrine embodied in a way of life, a method of leadership, a corrupt use of influence, and a hostile posture toward the faithful.

Second Timothy 3:1–5 provides a concentrated moral description. Love of self sits near the center. From there flow love of money, arrogance, slander, lack of self-control, brutality, treachery, conceit, and devotion to pleasure over devotion to God. These are not random vices. They are the moral expression of a heart turned away from the truth. Likewise, 2 Peter 2 and Jude portray false teachers as greedy, sensual, unstable, and self-serving. Such men do not merely happen to teach error. Their error and their corruption feed one another. Because they reject the authority of God's truth, they also cast off the restraints of holiness. Because they deny the Master, they become servants of their own desires.

The ecclesial shape of antichrist appears in the repeated emphasis that these men arise "among you," slip in unnoticed, and seek to draw away disciples. They are not content to remain isolated. They want influence, platforms, followers, and recognition. They work upon congregations. They target the unstable. They exploit the careless. They disturb fellowship. They fracture unity grounded in truth and replace it with alliances grounded in error. In this way antichrist from within is parasitic. It feeds on the visible life of the church while attacking the truth that gives the church life.

This explains why John's instruction in 2 John 10–11 is so sharp. The church must not assist the spread of false teaching. There is a kind of misplaced kindness that becomes participation in evil. To bless a deceiver in his doctrinal rebellion is to join hands with antichrist against the truth of Christ. The congregation must therefore understand that doctrinal boundaries are not acts of cruelty. They are acts of fidelity to Christ, protection for His people, and obedience to apostolic command. True love does not welcome the destruction of the gospel into the house of God.

It also explains why the faithful must measure the health of a congregation not merely by activity, size, influence, or reputation, but by its relation to apostolic doctrine. A body may possess outward vigor and yet be spiritually endangered if it tolerates or platforms those who do not remain in the teaching of Christ. The presence of religious energy is not itself proof of faithfulness. Antichrist can be energetic. False teachers can be industrious. Apostasy can be organized. What matters is whether the congregation abides in the doctrine of Christ and refuses partnership with those who deny Him.

The overall portrait is therefore unmistakable. Antichrist is not merely an enemy outside the camp. It also emerges through apostasy, deception, false teaching, and hostility from within the professing community. It departs from apostolic truth, refuses the teaching of Christ, introduces destructive error, targets the flock, and turns against those who remain faithful. Its moral character is corrupt, its ecclesial conduct is divisive and predatory, and its theological posture is rebellious. John's teaching prepares the church to recognize this reality without confusion. The faithful must not imagine that all danger comes from openly unbelieving society. Some of the gravest dangers come dressed in religious speech, moving among the visible people of God, while steadily drawing hearts away from the true Christ. Wherever that pattern appears, the church must name it soberly, resist it firmly, and remain steadfast in the apostolic truth that alone preserves fellowship with the Father and with His Son, Jesus Christ.

Edward D. Andrews

Part Two: The Prophetic Background of the Antichristic Conflict

Chapter 5. Daniel's Prophetic Pattern: Little Horns, Blasphemous Kings, and the War Against the Holy Ones

Beastly Empire in Daniel

When the reader turns from John's letters to Daniel, he moves from the direct use of the word *antichrist* to the prophetic patterns that stand behind later New Testament teaching. Daniel does not use the term antichrist, yet he provides some of the most important background for understanding how organized opposition to Jehovah and His Anointed develops in history. In Daniel, worldly dominion is repeatedly portrayed as beastly, arrogant, violent, and hostile toward the people of God. This is not a minor feature of the book. It is woven into its structure. The kingdoms of men rise with impressive strength, but when viewed from heaven's perspective they are not noble and orderly. They are ravenous beasts. They devour, trample, blaspheme, and persecute. That prophetic portrayal is vital because it shows that rebellion against God does not remain private or merely philosophical. It takes institutional form. It becomes political, religious, military, and judicial. It organizes itself against truth.

Daniel 7 is central to this pattern. Daniel sees four great beasts coming up from the sea, each different from the others. The sea imagery itself suggests restlessness, upheaval, and the agitated mass of the nations. These beasts are successive kingdoms or imperial powers, and they are presented not according to human admiration but according to divine evaluation. Men praise empire for its grandeur, strength, and administrative sophistication. God unmasks empire in rebellion as beastly power. That is one of the strongest foundations for later biblical teaching about the final anti-God order. The kingdoms of men, when detached from submission to Jehovah, do not become neutral instruments. They become predatory structures of pride and oppression.

The fourth beast in Daniel 7 receives special attention because it is dreadful, terrifying, and exceedingly strong. It has large iron teeth, devours and crushes, and tramples what is left with its feet. This detail matters because Daniel is not merely sketching a general atmosphere of wickedness. He is describing a historical pattern in which political power turns savage against God's order. Human government is ordained by God for justice, but rebellious government becomes beastly when it exalts itself against divine authority. That is why Daniel's vision is so important for the rest of biblical prophecy. It establishes that the opposition to God's kingdom will not only be doctrinal or personal. It will also involve aggressive systems of dominion that seek to rule the earth while suppressing truth and crushing the holy ones.

The heavenly scene that follows in Daniel 7 is just as important as the beast imagery itself. Thrones are set in place. The Ancient of Days takes His seat. Judgment is given. Dominion is taken away from the beasts. The Son of Man receives kingdom, glory, and everlasting rule. These truths place a strict limit on every empire of rebellion. However monstrous the beasts may appear on earth, they are temporary. They rise only under divine permission, remain only for an appointed span, and fall by divine judgment. This limitation is essential to the prophetic pattern. Daniel does not teach that beastly power is ultimate. He teaches that it is real, dangerous, and temporarily dominant, but always under heaven's control. Later prophetic passages build upon that exact foundation. The enemies of God seem overwhelming for a season, yet they are never outside His decree, never beyond His reach, and never able to overturn His kingdom purpose.

This perspective must govern the entire chapter. Daniel is not offering detached political analysis. He is unveiling the moral and spiritual character of rebellious empire. Beastly dominion is empire severed from obedience to God, intoxicated with its own power, and willing to devour anyone who stands in its path. Once the church sees that pattern, it will better understand why later revelation speaks of a beastly order in the final conflict. The roots of that imagery are already here. Daniel teaches the reader to see government, dominion, and public power from heaven's perspective. What looks magnificent to men may in truth be monstrous before God.

The Little Horn and the Assault on Truth

Within Daniel's vision of beastly empire, special attention is given to the little horn. This figure appears first in Daniel 7:8 among the ten horns of the fourth beast. Though called "little" at the start, it becomes great in speech, influence, and destructive force. It has eyes like the eyes of a man and a mouth speaking great things. Later in Daniel 7:20–25 it is described as making war with the holy ones, prevailing against them for a time, and speaking words against the Most High. This little horn is one of the clearest prophetic portraits of concentrated arrogant opposition to God. It is not merely another king among kings. It embodies boastful self-exaltation, hostility to the people of God, and active assault on divine order.

The horn's mouth is especially important. Daniel repeatedly emphasizes speech. This ruler does not merely conquer by force; he also speaks with arrogance. His words are not neutral political declarations. They are expressions of pride against heaven. He magnifies himself in speech before he wages war in action. That detail prepares the reader for later biblical portrayals of evil powers that blaspheme God and deceive men through proud and lying claims. In Scripture, speech is often the overflow of the heart. The little horn speaks great things because he embodies great rebellion. His mouth reveals his soul. He is not content with dominion; he demands self-exaltation.

Daniel 8 develops the pattern further. The little horn in that chapter grows exceedingly great toward the south, toward the east, and toward the Beautiful Land. It grows even to the host of heaven and throws down some of the host and some of the stars, trampling them. It magnifies itself as great as the Prince of the host. It removes the regular burnt offering and throws truth to the ground. Whether one is tracing the near historical setting or the larger prophetic pattern, the central elements are unmistakable: arrogant expansion, desecration of worship, hostility to the people of God, and assault on truth itself. The evil ruler in Daniel is not merely ambitious in ordinary political terms. He reaches upward in blasphemous presumption. He directs himself against heaven and against everything on earth that bears God's claim.

The phrase in Daniel 8:12 that "truth was cast down to the ground" is especially valuable for the doctrinal trajectory of this book. It shows that persecution and blasphemy are bound to falsehood. Evil power does not attack the people of God while leaving divine truth untouched. It wages war on both. It wants to cast down the truth because truth exposes rebellion, judges pride, and preserves fidelity among the holy ones. Thus the little horn is not simply a military oppressor. He is an anti-truth ruler. He cannot tolerate worship as Jehovah ordained it or truth as Jehovah revealed it. This is part of Daniel's enduring prophetic pattern: the enemies of God assault worship, truth, and the covenant people together.

Daniel 8:23–25 describes another fierce-looking king who understands riddles, destroys to an extraordinary degree, and by his shrewdness causes deceit to succeed. He magnifies himself in his heart and destroys many while they are at ease. He even rises up against the Prince of princes, yet he is broken without human hand. Here again the features are concentrated and unforgettable. We see cunning joined to violence, deceit joined to success, self-exaltation joined to opposition to God, and final judgment coming not through ordinary human triumph but through divine intervention. That pattern runs straight forward into later biblical revelation. The enemies of God are not only brutal; they are deceptive. They do not only persecute; they manipulate. They do not only resist truth; they counterfeit power while setting themselves against the Prince appointed by heaven.

The little horn material therefore teaches several truths that are essential for what follows in the book. First, anti-God power often begins in seemingly small form yet grows in influence and insolence. Second, the same power that persecutes the holy ones also attacks truth and worship. Third, self-exaltation is at the core of the matter. Fourth, the triumph of such evil is limited and temporary. Fifth, divine judgment is certain. Daniel is not giving scattered images without connection. He is establishing a prophetic template: arrogant power rises, blasphemes, deceives, persecutes, desecrates, and falls under the judgment of God.

The Abomination That Causes Desolation

Daniel 11:21–35 adds another vital dimension to the pattern by presenting a contemptible ruler who seizes power through intrigue, profanes the sanctuary, removes the regular burnt offering, and sets up the abomination that causes desolation. Here the prophecy highlights not only imperial arrogance but also sacrilegious intrusion into the sphere of worship. That is critical. Evil power in Daniel does not remain satisfied with civil domination. It moves against the holy place, the holy order, and the worship of God. It seeks to defile what belongs to Jehovah. This is why the language of desolation is so severe. It describes devastation brought into the domain that ought to be marked by holiness.

The "abomination that causes desolation" is not just an offensive act in general. It is a polluting rebellion that brings devastation through desecration. It is the intrusion of idolatrous and blasphemous power into what is set apart for God. Daniel's concern is not antiquarian detail for its own sake. The prophecy reveals a recurring pattern in which ungodly rulers do not merely oppose the people of God from a distance. They invade the sphere of worship and seek to replace divine order with sacrilege. Later revelation depends on this pattern. Once Daniel has taught the reader to expect desecrating power, the reader is prepared to understand why Jesus warns about the abomination of desolation and why later prophetic texts describe organized opposition to true worship.

Daniel 11 also shows the dividing effect of such a crisis. Some act wickedly toward the covenant. Others know their God and display strength. Some fall by sword, flame, captivity, and plunder. Others receive a little help. The wise give understanding to many, though they themselves suffer. This aspect of the prophecy must not be overlooked, because it teaches that when desecrating power rises, the people of God are sifted and revealed. Crisis exposes loyalty. Some compromise. Some flatter. Some collaborate. Others remain steadfast and instruct many. Thus Daniel not only predicts the actions of the arrogant ruler; he also describes the moral testing of the covenant community under pressure. This pattern will remain significant in later chapters, because anti-God power does not merely destroy externally. It reveals where men stand.

The expression "those who know their God will display strength and take action" is particularly important in the flow of Daniel 11. The answer to desecration is not panic but steadfast knowledge of God. Those who know Jehovah are not untouched by suffering, but they are not conquered in soul. They endure, resist, instruct, and remain faithful. This means the Danielic pattern is not only a prophecy of evil. It is also a prophecy of perseverance. The rise of the desolating power becomes the setting in which the faithful are purified, refined, and made manifest. Daniel 12 continues that theme by speaking of a time of distress unlike any before it, yet also of deliverance for those found written in the book.

The desolation language in Daniel also teaches that wickedness reaches a peculiar intensity when it invades worship. Ordinary political tyranny is terrible enough, but sacrilegious tyranny is something more. It seeks to rewrite reality at the level of allegiance. It aims to recast what is holy, what is true, and what is worthy of obedience. Therefore the abomination that causes desolation is not merely an event of military conquest. It is the theological signature of power that refuses to remain within creaturely limits. It seeks to occupy the space that belongs to God. That is why it becomes so important for later revelation. Daniel has already taught the church to recognize that evil matures when it becomes sacrilegious, blasphemous, and worship-corrupting.

The King Who Exalts Himself Above Every God

Daniel 11:36–39 gives one of the clearest portraits in the Old Testament of self-exalting rebellion. "The king will do according to his own will, and he will exalt and magnify himself above every god and will speak monstrous things against the God of gods." Whether one is discussing the near historical embodiment, the wider pattern, or the prophetic line that stretches forward, the description itself is unmistakable. Here is a ruler whose defining mark is self-exaltation. He does not simply reject a rival power. He lifts himself above every object of worship. He speaks against the God of gods. His issue is not only political ambition but religious usurpation. He wants supremacy in the realm of ultimate allegiance.

This is one of the most significant passages for the book's larger objective because it provides a deeply rooted Old Testament pattern of lawless self-deification. The king's rebellion is not modest. He does "according to his own will." He recognizes no higher authority above himself. That is the essence of lawlessness in its mature form. Lawlessness is not first social disorder in the common sense. It is refusal of God's authority. It is the creature enthroning his own will in defiance of the Creator. Daniel gives that revolt a face in the king who exalts himself above every god. Later biblical passages will use different vocabulary, but the pattern is already established here.

Daniel also says that this king will prosper "until the indignation is finished, because what is decreed will be done." That statement is immensely important. It means the rise of arrogant rebellion is neither random nor ultimate. The self-exalting king operates only within the boundary of divine decree. He prospers for a season because God has appointed that season for His own righteous purposes. But once the indignation is complete, the king's span is over. This guards the reader from despair. The ruler's success is real, but it is not sovereign. His boastful career is temporary, measured, and destined for judgment.

The imagery of arrogant ascent in Isaiah 14:12–15 and Ezekiel 28:1–10, while addressed in their own contexts to proud earthly rulers, throws further light on this recurring pattern. In Isaiah 14 the proud one says in his heart, "I will ascend to heaven; I will raise my throne above the stars of God." In Ezekiel 28 the ruler of Tyre says, "I am a god; I sit in the seat of gods," though he is a man and not God. These passages should not be flattened into identical prophecies, but they do reinforce the same moral profile found in Daniel: human rulers swollen with pride, aspiring beyond creaturely limits, speaking as though divinity belonged to them, and being cast down by divine judgment. The Bible repeatedly unmasks such arrogance as madness. When men attempt to seize what belongs to God, they reveal not greatness but doomed rebellion.

Daniel 11:36–39 therefore provides a concentrated portrait of the self-exalting ruler that later prophetic texts can echo without contradiction. The essential elements are already in place: unrestrained self-will, blasphemous speech, contempt for proper worship, temporary prosperity under divine limit, and final downfall. The church does not need to manufacture these ideas from later texts alone. Daniel has already laid the foundation. The mature anti-God ruler is a blasphemous usurper who magnifies himself against heaven.

The War Against the Holy Ones Under Divine Limit

Daniel's prophetic pattern is never only about the arrogance of rulers. It is also about the suffering and vindication of the holy ones. In Daniel 7:21 the little horn makes war with the holy ones and prevails against them for a time. In Daniel 7:25 he speaks against the Most High and wears down the holy ones of the Supreme One. In Daniel 8 the host is trampled. In Daniel 11 the wise fall by sword and flame, captivity and plunder. In Daniel 12 a time of distress comes unlike any before it. These descriptions are meant to sober the reader. Faithfulness to Jehovah does not exempt His people from intense opposition. On the contrary, the very rise of anti-God power often sharpens the conflict around the holy ones because they represent an allegiance the beastly order cannot tolerate.

Yet Daniel is equally clear that this warfare takes place under divine limit. The horn prevails only "until" the Ancient of Days comes and judgment is given. The oppression continues for an appointed time, times, and half a time. The regular burnt offering is removed for a measured duration. The distress is terrible, yet Michael stands up and deliverance comes. Again and again Daniel teaches that the suffering of the holy ones is real but bounded. Evil is permitted a span, not a throne over eternity. The same God who reveals the rise of arrogant rulers also reveals their limits. This truth will become crucial when later prophetic passages describe intensified oppression. The reader who has learned Daniel's pattern will know that temporary domination never means ultimate victory.

The phrase "wear out the holy ones" in Daniel 7 is especially revealing. Evil power often seeks not only to kill but to exhaust. It uses pressure, attrition, and prolonged oppression in an effort to erode faithfulness. This too belongs to the prophetic pattern. The anti-God order wages war not simply by open force but by wearing down the people of God through sustained conflict. That is why endurance becomes such a repeated biblical theme. The holy ones are called not merely to survive a single moment of danger but to persevere through prolonged pressure while waiting for God's appointed judgment.

Daniel 12 adds another vital note by speaking of purification. "Many will be cleansed, whitened, and refined." This does not mean the distress comes from God as a cruel experiment. Rather, it means Jehovah overrules the malice of wicked powers for the sanctification of His people. The oppressor intends destruction; God accomplishes purification. The arrogant ruler seeks to extinguish truth; God preserves a faithful remnant and gives understanding to the wise. This is one reason Daniel remains such a necessary foundation for later prophetic teaching. It does not simply identify evil. It teaches the people of God how to view history under pressure. The struggle is fierce, but the outcome is not in doubt.

How Daniel Prepares the Reader for Paul and Revelation

Daniel's visions create a prophetic vocabulary and pattern that later biblical writers can assume. He teaches the reader to recognize beastly empire, boastful rulers, persecution of the holy ones, desecration of worship, assault on truth, and temporary domination under divine decree. Once those themes are understood, the reader is prepared to follow later revelation without confusion. Paul's description of a self-exalting lawless figure and Revelation's portrayal of beastly anti-God power do not appear out of nowhere. They stand downstream from Daniel's prophetic world.

Daniel prepares the reader first by showing that rebellious dominion is beastly before God. That makes later beast imagery intelligible. He prepares the reader further by presenting rulers whose speech is blasphemous and whose hearts are lifted up against heaven. That makes later descriptions of arrogant anti-God figures intelligible. He prepares the reader again by showing that hostility to God's people and desecration of worship are part of the same pattern. That makes later depictions of persecuting and deceptive powers intelligible. Above all, he prepares the reader by insisting that such powers are judged, limited, and finally replaced by the everlasting kingdom of the Son of Man.

It is therefore unnecessary and unwise in this chapter to settle every historical question tied to Daniel's near fulfillments. Those details matter in their proper place, but the primary aim here is to identify the prophetic pattern that feeds forward into the rest of Scripture. Daniel gives the church the grammar of anti-God dominion. He teaches us what to watch for: boastful speech, self-exaltation, hatred of the holy ones, desecration of worship, trampling of truth, deceitful success, temporary power, and certain judgment. With that grammar in place, later chapters will be able to examine Pauline and Johannine passages without forcing them into artificial categories.

The church should therefore read Daniel as the foundational prophetic sketch of concentrated rebellion against Jehovah and His kingdom order. Daniel does not yet use all the later terminology, but he establishes the essential profile. The enemies of God do not simply disbelieve in private. They organize, speak, legislate, persecute, blaspheme, and seek to occupy the realm of worship and allegiance. They rise from the sea of the nations as beastly powers. They magnify themselves against heaven. They wear down the holy ones. They cast truth to the ground. They set up desolating abominations. They prosper for a measured season. Then they are broken without human hand.

That last point must remain fixed in the mind of the reader. Daniel's purpose is not to enthrone evil in the imagination of believers, but to teach them how evil looks from heaven and how it ends under judgment. The Ancient of Days still sits enthroned. The Son of Man still receives dominion. The kingdom still belongs in the end to the holy ones of the Supreme One. Every little horn, every blasphemous king, every desolating oppressor, and every beastly empire rises only for a season under divine limit. Daniel therefore gives the church not only a prophetic warning but also a prophetic framework of confidence. Evil may be fierce, but it is never final.

Chapter 6. The Messiah Opposed: False Christs, Desecration, and the Nations in Rebellion

The Nations Rage Against Jehovah and His Anointed

Psalm 2 stands as one of the clearest Old Testament declarations that opposition to the Messiah is not an accidental feature of history but a defining characteristic of the rebellious nations. The psalm opens with the question, "Why do the nations rage and the peoples meditate on an empty thing?" The kings of the earth take their stand, and rulers gather together "against Jehovah and against His Anointed." That language forms the theological foundation for everything Jesus later says about false christs, persecution, and end-time deception. The hostility of the nations toward the Messiah is not first explained as political calculation, cultural friction, or human misunderstanding. It is rebellion against Jehovah's appointed King. Men do not merely dislike certain moral teachings or resist one religious movement among many. They reject the authority of the One whom Jehovah has installed on Zion, His holy mountain.

This point is crucial because it prevents the church from misreading the conflict as merely horizontal. The opposition is vertical before it is horizontal. The nations rage because they do not want Jehovah's rule mediated through His Anointed. Their words in Psalm 2 reveal the motive of their hearts: "Let us tear their bonds apart and cast away their cords from us." The problem is not that the Messiah has done evil. The problem is that rebellious humanity does not want divine restraint, divine rule, divine truth, or divine claims over its life. The Messiah becomes intolerable to the world because He embodies Jehovah's kingship in history. To reject Him is therefore to reject God's order itself.

Psalm 2 also shows that this rebellion is organized. The kings "take their stand." The rulers "gather together." Opposition to the Messiah is not merely scattered irritation. It forms itself into policy, alliance, counsel, and public resistance. This must be remembered throughout the present chapter, because Jesus' warnings about false christs and desolating sacrilege do not appear in a vacuum. They unfold in the same world Psalm 2 already describes, a world in which rulers, powers, and peoples set themselves against Jehovah and His Christ. The Messiah is opposed not only by isolated individuals but by wider structures of human rebellion.

Yet the psalm also places that rebellion under divine scorn and judgment. He who sits in the heavens laughs; Jehovah holds them in derision. He then speaks in His wrath and announces the certainty of His decree: "I have installed My King upon Zion, My holy mountain." This means the nations do not create a real alternative kingdom. They rage under a sentence already fixed by heaven. Their resistance is real, but it is doomed. The Messiah will receive the nations as His inheritance and the ends of the earth as His possession. He will break rebellious opposition with a rod of iron. Thus Psalm 2 teaches both the fury of the nations and the certainty of the Messiah's victory. The church must keep both truths together. To see only the rage is to become fearful. To see only the victory without the rage is to become naïve. Scripture gives both.

This psalm also explains why messianic opposition inevitably extends to messianic followers. If the rulers of the earth hate Jehovah's Anointed, they will also hate those who bear His name, obey His Word, and submit to His kingship. Christ and His people cannot be separated in the world's hostility. That truth will appear more fully later in this chapter, but Psalm 2 already supplies the logic. Rebellion against the King includes rebellion against the kingdom community. The nations do not merely dispute a doctrine; they resist the reign of Jehovah mediated through His Son.

The closing exhortation of Psalm 2 is equally important. Kings are told to show insight, to be warned, to serve Jehovah with fear, and to kiss the Son lest He become angry. This shows that the psalm is not merely a sentence of doom but also a call to submission. The Son is not only the Judge of rebellious nations; He is the rightful object of allegiance. The nations are therefore without excuse. Their rage is not forced upon them. It is a chosen revolt against the One to whom every ruler owes obedience. This clarifies the moral nature of opposition to Christ. It is not neutral political resistance. It is culpable rebellion against Jehovah's enthroned Messiah.

False Christs and False Prophets

When Jesus speaks in Matthew 24, Mark 13, and Luke 21, He brings the prophetic pattern of Psalm 2 and Daniel into direct application for His disciples. One of His first warnings concerns false christs and false prophets. In Matthew 24:4–5 He says, "See that no one misleads you. For many will come in my name, saying, 'I am the Christ,' and they will mislead many." Mark 13:5–6 echoes the same warning, and Luke 21:8 adds that believers must not go after such men. This is highly significant. Before Jesus speaks of wars, desecration, tribulation, and public upheaval, He warns against deception centered on His own messianic identity. The attack falls first on truth about the Messiah.

That warning harmonizes perfectly with the material already established in John's letters. The doctrinal lie of antichrist is ultimately a lie about Christ. Jesus Himself prepares the church for that reality. False christs do not merely arise in a random religious marketplace. They emerge in relation to the true Messiah and seek to displace Him, imitate Him, or redirect allegiance away from Him. They are false precisely because they stand over against the real Christ while trading on messianic expectation. In that sense, Jesus' warning provides the soil from which John's later antichrist language grows. John gives the doctrinal category; Jesus gives the prophetic warning that such deceivers will come.

The plural language in the Gospels is also important. Jesus does not say only one deceiver will arise. He says "many" will come. That keeps the reader from reducing the entire subject of messianic opposition to one isolated personality. The history of the church includes repeated outbreaks of false claims, counterfeit leaders, false prophets, and deceptive religious movements. The danger is not imaginary, and it is not remote. It is woven into the age between Christ's first coming and His return. The church must therefore remain watchful not only against persecution from outside but also against counterfeit spirituality claiming divine authority.

Matthew 24:11 strengthens the point further: "Many false prophets will arise and mislead many." False christs and false prophets belong together because false messianic claims require false religious voices to support, justify, and spread them. Deception does not flourish without proclamation. Error seeks heralds. That is why Jesus warns not only about public claimants to messianic status but also about the wider network of deceptive voices that accompany them. This prepares the reader to see later prophetic developments more clearly. Whenever the truth about Christ is displaced, there will be agents of religious deception to legitimize that displacement.

Jesus returns to the warning in Matthew 24:23–25: "If anyone says to you, 'Look, here is the Christ,' or 'There He is,' do not believe it. For false christs and false prophets will arise and will perform great signs and wonders, so as to mislead, if possible, even the chosen ones. See, I have told you beforehand." Mark 13:21–23 says the same in nearly identical form. These words show that deception can be persuasive, dramatic, and externally impressive. Falsehood does not always appear weak or obviously ridiculous. It may come with signs, claims of power, and appeals to visible evidence. Yet Christ says plainly, "do not believe it." The standard is not spectacle but the Word He has already given.

This remains a needed corrective. Believers can become fascinated by signs, dramatic personalities, and urgent claims that a hidden or newly manifested messiah has appeared somewhere. Jesus shuts the door on that entire mentality. He tells His disciples beforehand so that they will not be swept up in the religious theater of deception. The church does not need secret knowledge or fresh claims beyond the apostolic witness. It needs steadfast adherence to the Christ who has already come, already spoken, already died, already risen, and who will return openly in His appointed hour.

False christs therefore reveal more than human confusion. They reveal active opposition to the Messiah. They are counterfeit rivals to the Son whom Jehovah has installed as King. They exploit religious expectation while denying the true identity, authority, and exclusivity of Jesus Christ. In this way the Gospels connect directly to the Johannine doctrine of antichrist. What Jesus warned about in prophetic discourse John later names with doctrinal precision. The church must hear both voices together.

The Desecrating Pattern in Jesus' Prophecy

Jesus does not merely warn against false teachers and false christs in the abstract. He explicitly directs His disciples back to Daniel when He speaks of desecration. In Matthew 24:15 He says, "Therefore when you see the abomination of desolation which was spoken of through Daniel the prophet, standing in the holy place…" Mark 13:14 likewise refers to "the abomination of desolation standing where it ought not." This is a decisive link between Daniel's prophetic pattern and Jesus' own teaching. Our Lord does not treat Daniel's visions as closed relics of a forgotten age. He treats them as a prophetic pattern with continuing significance. The desecrating outrage Daniel described remains part of the church's interpretive framework.

This link matters greatly for the doctrine of antichristic opposition. Daniel had already taught that arrogant power seeks not only political domination but sacrilegious intrusion into the sphere of worship. It profanes what belongs to God. Jesus confirms that the same pattern remains relevant. The battle over messianic allegiance inevitably involves desecration, that is, the invasion of holy space, holy order, or holy worship by anti-God power. Rebellion matures when it no longer contents itself with external resistance but seeks to occupy the realm that belongs to God alone.

The expression "abomination of desolation" carries both moral and covenantal force. It is not merely something unpleasant or politically offensive. It is something detestable before God that produces devastation in relation to His worship and covenant order. Jesus' appeal to Daniel shows that His disciples must understand history theologically. They must see that anti-Messianic power often reaches a sharper intensity when it becomes sacrilegious. A ruler or movement may begin in political pride, but the deeper pattern reveals itself when it seeks to profane what belongs to Jehovah.

The practical effect of Jesus' warning is also noteworthy. He speaks so that His disciples may discern and respond. Prophecy is given not to produce idle speculation but to cultivate vigilance. The church must recognize that deception and desecration are related. False christs prepare men to accept false worship. False prophets prepare men to tolerate sacrilege. Once truth concerning the Messiah is corrupted, the way is opened for deeper profanation. That is why Jesus joins warnings about deception with reference to Daniel's desecrating pattern. The corruption of truth and the corruption of worship advance together.

At the same time, Jesus' use of Daniel prevents shallow interpretation. The church must not think of desecration only in terms of crude violence while ignoring the theological issue underneath. The heart of desecration is usurpation. It is the replacement of what God ordained with what rebellion invents. It is the intrusion of anti-God claims into the space reserved for divine honor. In that sense, the desecrating pattern is broader than one isolated event. It is a recurring prophetic pattern that reaches its full intensity wherever anti-Messianic power invades the sphere of worship and allegiance.

This is why Jesus' appeal to Daniel serves as bridge material for the larger argument of the book. Daniel had already established the pattern of sacrilegious rulers, persecuting dominion, and temporary triumph under divine limit. Jesus takes that pattern and places it before His disciples as a lens through which to understand the coming age of conflict. The Messiah is opposed not only by unbelief in general but by false claimants, corrupt religious voices, and desecrating powers that seek to occupy what belongs to God. The church, therefore, must read history with prophetic sobriety rather than with worldly naïveté.

Persecution as a Mark of Messianic Opposition

Opposition to the Messiah does not remain confined to doctrinal distortion and sacrilegious intrusion. It also expresses itself in hatred toward those who belong to Him. Jesus makes this clear in John 15:18–21: "If the world hates you, you know that it has hated me before it hated you." Because believers are no part of the world, the world hates them. That hatred is not accidental. It flows from hostility to Christ Himself. The church must therefore understand persecution as one of the marks of messianic opposition. When men reject the King, they also resist His subjects. When they hate the Son, they also hate those who bear witness to Him.

This truth belongs naturally with Psalm 2 and the Olivet Discourse. The nations rage against Jehovah and His Anointed. False christs arise to displace the real Christ. Desecrating power invades the holy sphere. It follows that the faithful, who remain loyal to the Messiah, will become targets. The conflict is covenantal and kingdom-centered. Believers suffer not merely because they are inconvenient citizens of a troubled world, but because their allegiance to Jesus Christ exposes rebellion against Him. Their witness is intolerable to a system that does not want Jehovah's cords or the Son's authority.

IDENTIFYING THE ANTICHRIST

Jesus' warnings in Matthew 24 and Mark 13 include this theme of persecution. The disciples will be handed over to tribulation. They will be hated by all nations because of His name. Some will stumble, betray one another, and hate one another. This language shows that the rise of falsehood and the rise of pressure against the faithful belong to the same prophetic landscape. Deception and persecution advance side by side. False christs mislead many, and hostile powers oppress those who remain loyal to the true Christ. The church must not treat those as unrelated concerns. They are two aspects of one anti-Messianic struggle.

Persecution also reveals the moral nature of opposition to Christ. False teachers often present themselves as more enlightened, more inclusive, or more spiritually advanced than the faithful. But when the faithful refuse their lies, the mask slips. Hostility emerges. Slander intensifies. Pressure increases. The issue was never simply intellectual disagreement. It was rebellion against the truth. This is why Jesus does not tell His disciples merely to expect misunderstanding. He tells them to expect hatred. Messianic opposition is not neutral. It is animated by rebellion against the Son.

Yet persecution, like every other expression of anti-God power, operates under divine limit. Jesus warns His disciples beforehand, not to terrify them but to steady them. He wants them to know that such hatred confirms rather than disproves their union with Him. If the world had loved them as its own, that would have signaled a more dangerous compromise. Hatred from the world, though painful, testifies that believers belong to another kingdom. This does not make persecution easy, but it does give it meaning. It is one of the recurring marks that the Messiah is opposed and that His followers are joined to Him in that conflict.

The church should therefore recognize that anti-Messianic power can be measured not only by what it says about Christ but also by how it treats Christ's people. Falsehood eventually seeks conformity. Rebellion eventually seeks suppression of faithful witness. Anti-God systems do not rest until the testimony of the true Christ is silenced or marginalized. This is why endurance remains so central in the New Testament. Believers are called not merely to identify deception but to stand under pressure without abandoning the Son. Persecution becomes one of the places where true allegiance is manifested.

The Gathering of Kings Against the Returning Christ

The prophetic trajectory established in Psalm 2, Daniel, and Jesus' warnings reaches one of its clearest later expressions in Revelation 17:12–14 and Revelation 19:11–21. Revelation 17 describes ten kings who receive authority for one hour with the beast. These have one mind, and they give their power and authority to the beast. Then comes the decisive statement: "These will wage war against the Lamb, and the Lamb will conquer them, because He is Lord of lords and King of kings." This is Psalm 2 brought to its climactic expression. The rulers of the earth align themselves against Jehovah's Anointed. Their rebellion becomes coordinated, beast-supported, and openly hostile to the Messiah. Yet the outcome is never in doubt. The Lamb conquers.

This passage is highly important as bridge material because it shows that the rage of the nations is not merely an ancient pattern and not merely a first-century reality. It reaches a final concentration in the gathering of kings against Christ. The war against the Lamb is the ultimate unveiling of what has always been true of rebellious power. The nations do not simply want autonomy in the abstract. They do not want the Lamb to reign. They do not want the Messiah's rule. Therefore, they assemble themselves in defiance of His kingship. The same spirit that animated Psalm 2 appears here in concentrated form.

Revelation 19:11–21 then portrays the public answer from heaven. Christ appears riding a white horse, called Faithful and True. In righteousness He judges and wages war. His eyes are like a flame of fire. He is clothed in a robe dipped in blood. His name is called the Word of God. From His mouth comes a sharp sword with which to strike the nations, and He will shepherd them with a rod of iron. The deliberate echoes of Psalm 2 are unmistakable. The Son whom the nations rejected now appears in undeniable majesty as the warrior King. The rebellious kings, the beast, and the armies gathered against Him are decisively overthrown.

This scene shows the end of all anti-Messianic rebellion. False christs will not prevail. Desecrating powers will not prevail. The kings of the earth in their organized hostility will not prevail. The Messiah whom men denied, opposed, mocked, and resisted returns openly to judge and to reign. That is why every earlier warning in Scripture must be heard under the light of Christ's final victory. The church is not being prepared for defeat, but for endurance in the certainty of triumph. The Lamb conquers because He is who He is: Lord of lords and King of kings.

It is also important to notice that those with Him are "called and chosen and faithful" in Revelation 17:14. The faithful are not forgotten in the final conflict. Those who refused false christs, rejected deception, endured persecution, and remained loyal to the Lamb are identified with Him in victory. This reinforces the practical purpose of prophecy. The church is not called to fascination with evil but to fidelity to Christ. Scripture reveals the gathering of kings against the Lamb so that believers may know that the present rage of the nations belongs to a larger conflict already destined to end in the Messiah's triumph.

The chapter, then, serves its bridge purpose clearly. Psalm 2 establishes the rebellion of nations against Jehovah and His Anointed. Jesus warns of false christs, false prophets, and desecrating patterns drawn from Daniel. He teaches that hatred of His followers is an inevitable outworking of hatred toward Him. Revelation then shows that these patterns culminate in a final gathering of kings against the Lamb, only to be crushed by His appearing. The line is straight and the meaning is plain. The Messiah is opposed throughout history by deceptive religion, sacrilegious power, persecuting hatred, and rebellious rulers. Yet every strand of that opposition moves toward one end: public destruction before the returning Christ. The church must therefore read all present hostility in the light of that final certainty. The nations may rage, the deceivers may multiply, and the kings of the earth may gather, but Jehovah has already installed His King, and the Lamb will conquer all who set themselves against Him.

Edward D. Andrews

Part Three: Paul's Doctrine of the Great Apostasy and the Man of Lawlessness

Chapter 7. The Great Apostasy Before the Day of the Lord

The Thessalonian Crisis and Paul's Correction

Second Thessalonians 2:1–5 opens in the middle of a pastoral crisis. The believers in Thessalonica had become disturbed about "the coming of our Lord Jesus Christ and our gathering together to Him." Paul's language shows that the matter was not abstract. It was affecting the congregation's stability. They were being shaken in mind and alarmed, apparently by claims that the day of the Lord had already arrived or was immediately present in some realized sense. Whether the pressure came through a supposed spiritual utterance, a spoken report, or a forged letter, the effect was the same: the congregation was unsettled. Paul therefore writes not to feed prophetic excitement, but to restore order, sobriety, and fidelity to apostolic truth. That alone is an important beginning for this chapter. A proper doctrine of apostasy does not arise from feverish speculation. It arises from careful attention to what the apostle actually says in order to correct confusion.

Paul's correction is deliberate and exact. He does not simply tell the Thessalonians to calm down. He gives them doctrinal structure. He says that certain things must occur before the day they feared had already arrived. This means prophetic confusion is answered by revealed sequence, not by emotional reassurance alone. The church is not left to spiritual rumor, private impressions, or religious excitement. It is bound to apostolic teaching. Paul had already instructed them on these matters when He was with them, and now He recalls that earlier teaching so they may not be carried away by deceptive claims. That is an important mark of true biblical Christianity. It returns to the apostolic Word. Mere outward profession is easily swept along by reports, sensations, and claims of special insight. Genuine faith is steadied by what the apostles taught from the beginning.

This passage also reveals the danger of religious deception within the professing sphere. The problem was not merely that hostile pagans opposed the congregation. The deeper problem was that misleading influence had entered the church's hearing and disturbed its understanding of Christ's coming. That pattern is essential to this chapter. The great apostasy Paul describes is not first a matter of the world becoming immoral, though the world is immoral. It is a matter of religious confusion and defection pressing upon those who outwardly stand in relation to Christian truth. The Thessalonian crisis therefore prepares the reader to understand apostasy rightly. Paul is not addressing secular decline in general. He is addressing deception touching the church's confession, hope, and doctrinal stability.

The apostle's words also teach us how believers must respond when prophetic matters become a source of agitation. They must not build their expectations on every dramatic claim. Paul explicitly says, in effect, do not let anyone deceive you. That command governs the entire section. Before he identifies the apostasy and the man of lawlessness, he establishes the moral necessity of discernment. Christians must resist the temptation to grant authority to whatever sounds urgent, spiritual, or dramatic. The apostolic standard remains decisive. What has Christ's apostle actually taught? What accords with revealed truth? What keeps the church anchored in the promises of God rather than tossed about by fear? A congregation that loses that anchoring becomes vulnerable not merely to mistaken chronology but to a deeper revolt from truth itself.

The opening verses therefore frame the doctrine of apostasy in a distinctly ecclesial way. The issue arises in relation to the church's understanding of Christ's return. The correction comes through apostolic authority. The danger involves deception rather than simple ignorance. The solution is not hidden knowledge but remembering what Paul had taught them. Already the line is being drawn between authentic Christianity and nominal profession. True Christianity submits to apostolic revelation. Nominal religion may speak much about Christ's coming while being ready to abandon apostolic boundaries whenever a more dramatic message appears. Paul will not permit that. He calls the church back to the truth that had already been entrusted to it.

The Apostasy Must Come First

Paul's next statement is one of the decisive declarations in the whole chapter: "that day will not come unless the apostasy comes first." The wording is direct and weighty. Paul does not describe a minor fluctuation in public religion. He speaks of "the apostasy," a falling away so definite and so significant that it stands as a marked event or condition in relation to the day of the Lord. This alone shows that apostasy in Scripture is not a light word. It is not synonymous with temporary discouragement, confusion over secondary matters, or every act of inconsistency in the life of professing believers. Paul is describing a deliberate revolt from revealed truth.

The nature of this revolt becomes clear when the wider New Testament witness is considered alongside 2 Thessalonians 2. Acts 20:29–30 records Paul's warning that savage wolves would enter among the flock and that from among the elders' own number men would arise speaking twisted things to draw away disciples after themselves. First Timothy 4:1 says some will fall away from the faith by paying attention to deceitful spirits and teachings of demons. Second Timothy 4:3–4 says a time will come when men will not endure sound teaching, but wanting their ears tickled, they will accumulate teachers according to their own desires and turn away from the truth to myths. Second Peter 2:1 speaks of false teachers arising "among you," secretly introducing destructive heresies. When these texts are read together, the meaning of apostasy becomes unmistakable. It is not the ordinary unbelief of the pagan world. It is defection from the truth once heard, once professed, and once publicly associated with the Christian congregation.

This is why the apostasy must be located within the professing Christian sphere. The unbelieving world has always been alienated from God. It cannot "fall away" from apostolic truth in the same way as those who have stood under its hearing and outward profession. Apostasy requires proximity to revelation. It is departure, not mere distance. It is revolt, not mere ignorance. It is abandonment of what was once acknowledged, at least externally. Hebrews 3:12 warns professing believers to take care lest there be in any one of them an evil heart of unbelief in falling away from the living God. Hebrews 10:38–39 contrasts drawing back to destruction with faith preserving the soul. Those warnings confirm that apostasy belongs to the realm of covenant hearing and outward identification. It is the sin of turning from the light once received.

That distinction is essential for the objective of this book. True biblical Christianity must be clearly separated from mere outward profession. Not everyone who moves among Christian language, assemblies, institutions, and practices truly belongs to Christ. Paul's doctrine of apostasy makes that plain. A person may profess faith, receive instruction, and stand among believers outwardly, yet later reject sound teaching and defect into error. The falling away reveals what the heart loves. If the truth of Christ is abandoned for more pleasing doctrine, easier morality, self-exalting leadership, or spiritually seductive error, that is not development within Christianity. It is apostasy from Christianity.

The phrase "must come first" also shows that the apostasy is not accidental or peripheral. It has a fixed place in the prophetic order.

Paul is not merely predicting that some people will always drift. He is identifying a significant rebellion that prepares the stage for what follows. The falling away is therefore both a moral and prophetic reality. Morally, it is treachery against revealed truth. Prophetically, it is part of the unfolding pattern before the day of the Lord. The church must hear both aspects. Apostasy is not simply unfortunate decline; it is rebellion with eschatological significance.

A Religious Revolt, Not Mere Secular Decline

One of the most serious mistakes in handling this passage is to equate the apostasy with secular society becoming more immoral, irreligious, or hostile to biblical values. The moral decay of the world is real, but Paul's wording reaches in another direction. The apostasy is a religious revolt. It concerns those who stand in some outward relation to the truth and then abandon it. It belongs in the realm of confession, teaching, worship, and allegiance. That is why the church must not satisfy itself with general observations about cultural decline while missing the more searching warning directed toward the professing Christian sphere.

The supporting texts make this point again and again. First Timothy 4:1–3 describes people who pay attention to deceitful spirits and teachings of demons while still moving in the realm of religion. These are not straightforward atheists. They are propagators of spiritually framed error. Second Timothy 4:3–4 describes people who do not endure sound teaching and who gather teachers according to their own desires. Again, the issue is not simple worldliness from afar. It is rejection of sound doctrine while retaining enough religious appetite to seek other teachers. Second Peter 2:1 says false teachers secretly introduce destructive heresies "among you." The apostasy is therefore ecclesial before it is societal. It is a revolt within the visible sphere of religion.

This understanding sheds light on why apostasy is so dangerous. Secular unbelief is often easier to identify because it openly rejects the authority of Scripture. Religious apostasy is more deceptive because it often keeps Christian terminology while severing itself from Christian truth. It may still speak about God, Jesus, grace, worship, church, and spirituality. It may still preserve forms, ceremonies, offices, and claims of continuity. Yet if it no longer endures sound teaching, no longer remains in apostolic doctrine, and no longer bows to the truth concerning Christ, it is not biblical Christianity. It is revolt concealed beneath profession. That is precisely why Paul's warning is necessary. Outward form can survive long after inward fidelity has died.

The phrase "mere outward profession" must therefore be taken with full seriousness. Outward profession includes all the visible features by which a person or body appears Christian before men while lacking steadfast submission to apostolic truth. It may involve attendance, ritual, official position, inherited identity, verbal confession, or theological vocabulary. None of those things, by themselves, establish true Christianity. True biblical Christianity is marked by persevering faith in Christ, love for the truth, endurance in sound teaching, and obedience to the apostolic Word. Where those things are abandoned, no amount of institutional continuity can cancel the reality of apostasy.

This is also why the apostasy can grow large without becoming true. Numbers do not sanctify revolt. Antiquity does not sanctify revolt. Cultural prestige does not sanctify revolt. The religious revolt Paul foresees may gain influence, systems, teachers, and broad acceptance, but it remains rebellion because it departs from revealed truth. The church must be trained to judge religious claims by Scripture, not by size, success, sophistication, or public legitimacy. That is one of the practical burdens of this chapter. A body may look impressive before men and yet be in apostasy if it has abandoned the faith once delivered.

Paul's language compels the church to think with theological precision. The apostasy is not merely the background noise of a wicked age. It is a distinct religious falling away. It operates where Christ is named but not truly honored, where doctrine is professed but not endured, where teachers are multiplied not to preserve truth but to gratify desire, and where the visible sphere of Christianity becomes the setting for revolt against the apostolic faith. Until this is understood, the warning of 2 Thessalonians 2 will be reduced to general commentary on social decline and will lose its true edge.

The Falling Away From Apostolic Teaching

The New Testament repeatedly identifies apostasy with departure from apostolic teaching. This must remain central because Christianity is not a free religious movement in which each generation may redefine the faith according to its own preferences. It is grounded in a message revealed by God through Christ and delivered by His apostles. To fall away, therefore, is to depart from that deposit. It is to refuse the truth once proclaimed and to substitute another message more agreeable to fallen desire. Paul's supporting texts make this clear from several angles.

Acts 20:29–30 presents apostasy as the work of wolves who speak twisted things in order to draw away disciples after themselves. The goal is not loyalty to Christ as revealed by His apostles. The goal is allegiance to the false teachers. This is one of the clearest marks of apostasy from apostolic teaching: the center shifts from revealed truth to human influence. When teachers become the focal point, when charisma displaces doctrine, and when disciples are attached to personalities rather than to the apostolic gospel, the line of departure has already been crossed. Apostasy does not merely distort isolated details. It reorients allegiance.

First Timothy 4:1–3 identifies another aspect of the falling away: it occurs through attention to deceitful spirits and teachings of demons. That phrase should not be softened. Doctrinal revolt is not spiritually neutral. Behind false teaching stands a darker source. Demonic influence does not always appear in grotesque form. It can work through refined doctrine, religious severity, or counterfeit holiness. What marks it out is that it departs from the truth God has spoken. Thus apostasy from apostolic teaching is not simply an intellectual mistake. It is surrender to spiritually destructive error. The church must therefore test doctrine not by novelty or emotional appeal, but by conformity to the apostolic witness.

Second Timothy 4:3–4 adds the moral explanation for this revolt. People will not endure sound teaching because they want something else. They will accumulate teachers according to their own desires. The falling away from apostolic doctrine is therefore not merely imposed from the outside. It is welcomed by the flesh. Truth confronts sin, humbles pride, and demands submission to Christ. False teaching can be shaped to flatter the hearer instead. It may reduce holiness, blur judgment, magnify human ability, promise religious experience without obedience, or preserve a Christian name while removing biblical content. In that way apostasy spreads because it offers the religious world what the flesh prefers.

Hebrews 3:12 and Hebrews 10:38–39 bring out the inward root of the matter. Apostasy is tied to an evil heart of unbelief and to drawing back rather than persevering in faith. This shows again why true biblical Christianity must be distinguished from outward profession. Outward profession may continue for a time without a heart transformed by the truth. But when pressure, desire, false teaching, or fear intensify, the lack of real faith becomes manifest. The apostate draws back because he never truly loved the truth above all. Genuine believers certainly need warnings, and those warnings are one of the means Jehovah uses to preserve them. But the warnings also expose the difference between those who merely profess and those who truly endure.

Second Peter 2:1–3 gathers these strands into a single portrait. False teachers arise among the people, introduce destructive heresies, deny the Master, exploit others with false words, and bring destruction upon themselves. That description shows that apostasy from apostolic teaching is doctrinal, moral, and exploitative. It denies the rightful Master. It corrupts the flock. It traffics in falsehood. It pursues gain. The church must therefore refuse every attempt to make apostasy sound like an innocent theological broadening. The apostles speak of it as defection, denial, deception, and destruction.

For this reason, the line between true biblical Christianity and outward profession must be drawn where the apostles draw it: at perseverance in revealed truth. True Christianity abides in the apostolic doctrine concerning Christ. It receives sound teaching even when that teaching humbles and corrects. It endures under pressure rather than collecting teachers to satisfy desire. It clings to the Lord Jesus Christ as the apostles proclaimed Him. Outward profession may imitate many of those features for a season, but once the truth is no longer loved, endured, and obeyed, the profession collapses into apostasy.

Why the Apostasy Prepares the Way for the Lawless One

Paul's wording in 2 Thessalonians 2 shows that the apostasy and the revelation of the man of lawlessness belong together in ordered relationship. The apostasy comes first, and then the lawless one is revealed. This chapter must not yet treat the lawless one in full detail, but it must explain why the falling away prepares the way for him. The answer lies in the nature of apostasy itself. When apostolic truth is abandoned, the ground is cleared for counterfeit authority, false worship, and self-exalting rebellion. Lawlessness does not arise in a vacuum. It flourishes where truth has been surrendered.

Apostasy prepares the way for the lawless one by weakening the church's doctrinal defenses. As long as apostolic teaching is loved, guarded, and obeyed, there is resistance to false authority. But when sound doctrine is no longer endured, when teachers are chosen according to desire, and when the visible sphere of Christianity drifts from revealed truth, then the conditions are ripe for more concentrated rebellion. Men who no longer submit to Christ's Word are ready to submit to another voice. Once the truth is exchanged for pleasing error, the conscience has already been trained to receive what God did not authorize. The lawless one, therefore, does not merely appear before an intact church. He emerges in a context already prepared by revolt.

The apostasy also prepares the way by normalizing religious rebellion. The more the professing sphere tolerates departures from apostolic teaching, the less shocking further departures become. What once would have been recognized as intolerable can come to seem acceptable, then normal, then necessary. In this way revolt matures. Doctrinal compromise dulls discernment. Outward profession without inward fidelity creates a religious environment that can still speak

Christian language while being increasingly alien to biblical Christianity. That environment is fertile soil for lawlessness, because lawlessness is ultimately the enthronement of human will over divine revelation.

There is also a deeper theological connection. Apostasy rejects the authority of truth. The lawless one embodies rejection of authority in concentrated form. The one prepares for the other because both are expressions of rebellion against God, though one is broader and the other more focused. The apostasy is the larger falling away from revealed truth within the professing sphere. The lawless one is the unveiled concentration of self-exalting rebellion emerging in that context. Where the truth is not loved, a usurper can rise. Where the doctrine of Christ is not endured, counterfeit authority can claim sacred space. Where faithfulness has become nominal, lawlessness can present itself with greater confidence.

This is why the church must never treat apostasy as a secondary concern. It is not merely one problem among many. It is a preparatory revolt with far-reaching consequences. To abandon apostolic teaching is to open the door to greater deception. To preserve the form of Christianity while casting off its truth is to prepare the stage for deeper profanation. Paul's order is therefore profoundly instructive. Before the lawless one is revealed, the apostasy comes. The broad revolt creates the atmosphere in which the concentrated rebel can be manifested.

The practical lesson is urgent. The church must not imagine that it can tolerate serious doctrinal departure without inviting larger catastrophe. Every surrender of apostolic truth strengthens the conditions of lawlessness. Every elevation of human desire over sound doctrine weakens resistance to counterfeit authority. Every confusion of outward profession with genuine Christianity dulls the congregation's ability to distinguish truth from rebellion. The great apostasy is therefore not merely a subject for future speculation. It is a warning to guard the faith now, to endure sound teaching now, and to refuse every form of Christianity that keeps the name of Christ while abandoning His truth. Only a church anchored in apostolic doctrine will be prepared to face what comes after the falling away.

Chapter 8. The Man of Lawlessness Revealed

Why Paul Calls Him "the Man of Lawlessness"

When Paul writes of "the man of lawlessness" in 2 Thessalonians 2:3–4, He is not introducing a trivial label or an incidental detail within the prophecy. He is defining the essential character of the figure or reality He is describing. Lawlessness is not merely disorder in the common social sense, nor is it simply a refusal to obey civil rules. In the biblical sense, lawlessness is rebellion against God's authority. It is the creature refusing the Creator's right to rule. It is the rejection of revealed truth, revealed worship, and revealed boundaries. Therefore, when Paul speaks of "the man of lawlessness," He is describing the concentrated embodiment of revolt against Jehovah in the sphere where divine order ought to be honored.

That expression must be handled with care. Paul does not say merely that a lawless man exists somewhere in human history. He speaks of "the man of lawlessness" as a recognized manifestation of rebellion that becomes publicly revealed. This is why the present chapter must define him functionally and theologically, not merely as a political curiosity. In harmony with the broader prophetic pattern already established in Daniel and with the doctrinal line developed, the man of lawlessness is best understood not as a bare isolated ruler detached from institutional context, but as the concentrated, public expression of organized apostate rebellion. He is "man" in the sense of concentrated representation. He gathers into one visible form the mature character of rebellion that has already been developing in the professing sphere.

Paul's own context supports this understanding. The man of lawlessness is connected to "the apostasy" in 2 Thessalonians 2:3. The falling away comes first, and then the man of lawlessness is revealed. That sequence matters. It shows that the lawless one does not appear in a vacuum. He emerges in the setting of a religious revolt. The broader sphere of apostasy prepares for the more focused unveiling of lawlessness. This alone should warn the reader away from reducing the passage to a simplistic portrait of one secular dictator rising out of nowhere. Paul's concern is deeper. The revolt is religious before it is merely political. The lawlessness is aimed at the sphere of worship, truth, and divine claim. Therefore, the man of lawlessness is not merely anti-social. He is anti-God in an openly exalted way.

Daniel 11:36–39 provides essential background here. There the king "does according to his own will," exalts and magnifies himself above every god, and speaks monstrous things against the God of gods. That is the Old Testament pattern of mature lawlessness. The ruler's defining feature is not merely military strength, though power accompanies him. It is self-will lifted into the realm of worship. He will not remain within creaturely boundaries. He places his own will at the center. That is exactly what lawlessness means in its ripest form. The man of lawlessness is therefore the fully exposed embodiment of the principle already at work wherever men reject the authority of God's Word. He is lawlessness public, brazen, organized, and enthroned in the religious sphere.

This also explains why the church must not think of lawlessness as a purely moral problem detached from doctrine. Lawlessness is doctrinal because it refuses God's truth. It is ecclesial because it grows in relation to the professing sphere. It is institutional because it reaches public expression in structures of worship and authority. It is personal because it concentrates itself in a recognizable manifestation. And it is blasphemous because it seeks what belongs to God alone. Paul's wording is therefore extraordinarily precise. He is not describing random wickedness. He is naming the mature form of organized rebellion against Jehovah.

The Son of Destruction and the Judas Parallel

Paul adds another title in 2 Thessalonians 2:3: the man of lawlessness is "the son of destruction." This phrase deepens the portrait. It shows not only what he is morally, but what he is destined for judicially. He belongs to destruction. He is marked out by it. His character leads to it, and his end is fixed by it. In biblical language, to be called a "son of" something is often to be identified by its character or destiny. Thus the lawless one is not merely threatened with destruction in a general way. He is stamped by a doom appropriate to his nature. He is the son of destruction because destruction fits him, follows him, and claims him under divine judgment.

This expression immediately recalls John 17:12, where Jesus refers to Judas Iscariot as "the son of destruction." That parallel is highly instructive. Judas was not a pagan outsider attacking Christ from a distant throne. He arose from within the circle of profession. He moved among the disciples. He occupied a place of nearness to holy things. Yet he was false at the core. He betrayed the Lord under the cover of discipleship. That pattern sheds important light on the man of lawlessness. The Judas parallel suggests that the lawless one belongs not first to the sphere of obvious unbelief, but to the sphere of false profession and treacherous betrayal. He stands in relation to the house of God while opposing the God of the house.

This is exactly why the title "son of destruction" carries so much weight. Judas embodied betrayal within the sphere of covenant proximity. He was outwardly near, inwardly false, and finally exposed in ruin. In the same way, the man of lawlessness is not best understood as a merely external enemy operating wholly outside religious claims. He belongs to the realm of apostate profession. He is a usurping figure produced by revolt within the visible sphere of faith. Like Judas, he demonstrates that proximity to divine things is not the same as loyalty to divine truth. Like Judas, he represents treachery clothed in religious form. And like Judas, he moves toward certain destruction.

This parallel also guards the church from naïveté. It teaches that the gravest dangers often arise not from those who openly reject Christ from the start, but from those who stand close enough to sacred things to corrupt them from within. Judas did not need pagan office in order to become a betrayer. His position within the visible circle made the betrayal more severe. So too the man of lawlessness is not terrifying merely because of raw force, but because of sacrilegious nearness joined to sacrilegious rebellion. He does not simply stand outside the temple shouting blasphemies. He moves into the sphere where reverence ought to reign and exalts himself there.

The title "son of destruction" also assures the faithful that the end of lawlessness is certain. Paul is not describing an enemy whose fate remains unresolved. The lawless one may appear formidable for a season, but he is already named by his doom. He belongs to destruction because Jehovah has already determined the end of all usurping rebellion. This is crucial pastorally. The church must never treat the man of lawlessness as though he could finally succeed. His unveiling is real and serious, but so is his sentence. He bears the mark of ruin from the outset because nothing raised against God can endure.

Self-Exaltation in the Temple of God

Paul then gives the clearest functional description of the lawless one in 2 Thessalonians 2:4: he "opposes and exalts himself against every so-called god or object of worship, so that he sits in the temple of God, displaying himself as being God." This statement lies at the very center of the chapter. It identifies the lawless one by opposition, self-exaltation, intrusion, and usurpation. Each of those elements must be understood if the identity of the man of lawlessness is to be properly grasped.

First, he "opposes." The lawless one is not neutral toward God, Christ, truth, or worship. He is set against them. His posture is adversarial. Yet his opposition is not merely expressed in coarse unbelief. It takes the more dangerous form of sacrilegious intrusion. He does not remain content to deny from a distance. He moves into the sphere of worship itself. That is what makes the figure so severe. Open opposition is bad enough; usurping opposition in the house of God is far worse.

Second, he "exalts himself." This brings Paul into direct continuity with Daniel 11:36–39. The lawless one is marked by self-magnification. His issue is not only error; it is arrogant enthronement of the self. He raises himself over every so-called god or object of reverence. He cannot tolerate rival claims because lawlessness in mature form demands supremacy. It does not ask merely to coexist with the truth. It seeks to replace the truth's rightful authority with its own.

Third, he sits "in the temple of God." The phrase must be interpreted in a way consistent with Paul's context and the chapter's theological thrust. Since the lawless one arises in connection with the apostasy, and since his defining action concerns the sphere of worship, the strongest reading is that the "temple of God" here refers to the professing sphere that claims relation to God, not merely to a secular empire. Paul's burden is ecclesial and religious. He is describing a usurpation in the realm that outwardly belongs to God. This is not simply a tyrant ruling over unbelievers in a godless state. It is a sacrilegious enthronement in the house where divine honor ought to be preserved.

This is one reason Matthew 24:15 is such an important supporting text. Jesus speaks of "the abomination of desolation" standing in the holy place, drawing on Daniel's pattern of desecrating intrusion. Paul's language fits that same pattern. The man of lawlessness takes his place where he does not belong. He enters the sphere marked off for God and occupies it with self-exalting claims. He does not simply defy heaven from below; he invades the precincts of worship and seeks to redefine allegiance from within.

Fourth, he "displays himself as being God." This is the climax of the description. The lawless one is not merely corrupt administration in religion. He is not just a bad teacher among others. He is the public expression of institutionalized apostasy reaching the point of divine usurpation. He claims what belongs to God alone. Whether through office, prerogative, authority, worship, or practical claims of mediating supremacy, the essence is the same: he presents himself in the place of God. That is why this figure cannot be treated as a merely secular tyrant. Secular rulers may commit terrible injustices, but Paul's concern here is specifically with self-exaltation in the sphere of worship.

The church must therefore understand the "temple" statement as a theological unveiling of apostate religion at its height. The man of lawlessness is institutionalized rebellion becoming visibly enthroned where reverence for Jehovah should reign. He is the concentrated expression of apostasy becoming public, authoritative, and self-deifying. This is the mature form of what antichristic and apostate tendencies already point toward: the replacement of divine truth and divine authority with a human religious power that exalts itself as ultimate.

A Religious Usurper, Not a Mere Secular Tyrant

At this point the distinction must be stated plainly. The man of lawlessness is not best understood as merely one political despot ruling an empire from outside the sphere of faith. He is a religious usurper. That does not mean political elements are absent from later prophetic development, but in 2 Thessalonians 2 the accent falls on apostasy, temple, worship, self-exaltation, and divine usurpation. Paul's concern is not first civil administration. It is sacrilegious authority in the realm that claims relation to God.

This reading is supported by the chapter's flow. The lawless one is connected to the apostasy, not merely to international conflict. He sits in the temple of God, not merely on a political throne. He exalts himself over objects of worship, not merely over rival governments. These are religious and theological categories. The man of lawlessness therefore represents organized apostate rebellion becoming concentrated in a public, exalted, and worship-centered form. He is the mature flowering of what happens when the professing sphere abandons apostolic truth and yields itself to self-exalting authority.

Daniel 11:36–39 again clarifies the matter. The king exalts himself above every god and speaks monstrous things against the God of gods. He is not simply a civil leader making pragmatic decisions. He is a blasphemous usurper moving in the realm of worship. Paul draws on that same line. The lawless one is the New Testament counterpart to that Danielic pattern, now described in the context of apostasy before the day of the Lord. Therefore, the church should not cheapen the passage by reducing it to whatever secular strongman happens to terrify one generation or another. Paul is exposing a deeper religious rebellion.

The institutional dimension is also essential. The man of lawlessness is not a free-floating personality detached from all structure. He represents organized apostate power. The revolt has become embodied, public, and enthroned. This is why the singular expression "man" need not force the reader into an impoverished individualism. Scripture often uses singular forms representatively. The man of lawlessness can therefore be the concentrated public expression of a broader apostate order without losing his personal and visible features. In fact, that is what makes the title so forceful. He gathers into one public form the lawless character of an entire system of rebellion.

This understanding is in harmony with the line already developed in earlier chapters. Antichrist in John's writings is both plural and singular. Apostasy in Paul is a broad revolt within the professing sphere. The man of lawlessness is the unveiled concentration of that revolt. He is not disconnected from the broader antichristic phenomenon, but neither should he be carelessly collapsed into every other figure. His distinct role is to manifest institutionalized apostasy as self-exalting, temple-invading, God-usurping lawlessness. That is his theological identity.

This is why the church must be deeply cautious about religious power that lifts itself above Scripture, above apostolic doctrine, above accountability to Christ, and into claims that belong only to God. Wherever the visible sphere of religion begins to enthrone human authority in the place of divine authority, the pattern of lawlessness is already showing itself. The final concentration may reach fuller exposure later, but the character of it is already clear from Paul's description. It is usurpation in sacred space.

Destroyed by the Appearance of Christ's Coming

Paul completes the portrait in 2 Thessalonians 2:8: "then the lawless one will be revealed, whom the Lord Jesus will slay with the breath of His mouth and bring to nothing by the appearance of His coming." This verse is indispensable because it shows both the certainty of the lawless one's unveiling and the certainty of his destruction. The church must never study the man of lawlessness apart from the triumph of Christ. Evil is exposed in order to be judged, not merely admired for its dark complexity.

The phrase "the breath of His mouth" recalls Isaiah 11:4, where the Messianic ruler strikes the earth with the rod of His mouth and slays the wicked with the breath of His lips. This is no accidental echo. Paul is placing the lawless one under the authority of the promised Messianic Judge. The same Christ whose Word reveals truth will by that same sovereign power destroy the usurper. Lawlessness rises by arrogant speech, but it is ended by the greater speech of the Lord Jesus Christ. The false claimant exalts himself in the temple; the true Lord appears from heaven and reduces him to nothing.

Revelation 19:15 provides a similar picture. From the mouth of Christ comes a sharp sword with which He strikes the nations. Again the emphasis is on sovereign, judicial power proceeding from the Messiah Himself. The enemies of God do not fall because they are outmaneuvered by human brilliance. They fall because Christ appears. The lawless one is therefore not destroyed gradually by mere historical drift or institutional reform. He is decisively brought to nothing by the appearing of the Lord.

This is deeply significant for the identity of the man of lawlessness. His end is tied directly to the appearance of Christ's coming. That means his revealed form belongs to the final horizon of divine judgment. He is not simply one among many ordinary apostates whose memory fades with time. He is the public concentration of lawlessness brought onto the stage for direct destruction by the returning Christ. That alone shows why Paul treats him with such gravity. Yet the gravity is matched by certainty. The Lord Jesus destroys him. Not might destroy. Not perhaps overcome. He will slay and bring to nothing.

The church must draw strength from this. The lawless one may sit in the temple of God and display himself as being God, but he remains a creature under sentence. His claims are fraudulent, his authority is temporary, and his doom is fixed. The Lord Jesus does not struggle uncertainly against him. He destroys him by His appearing. The usurper's apparent majesty collapses the moment the rightful King is manifested. All false enthronement vanishes before the true Lord of glory.

This final note also protects the chapter from unhealthy fascination. The purpose of identifying the man of lawlessness is not to create fear-driven obsession. It is to sharpen discernment and strengthen loyalty to Christ. Paul reveals the character of the lawless one so the church may recognize the seriousness of apostasy, the sacrilege of usurping religious power, and the certainty of Christ's victory. The lawless one is real. His unveiling matters. His self-exaltation is blasphemous. But the last word is not his. The last word belongs to the Lord Jesus Christ, who by the appearance of His coming brings the entire lawless pretension to nothing.

Thus the man of lawlessness stands revealed in functional and theological terms. He is the concentrated, public expression of institutionalized apostate rebellion. He rises in connection with the great apostasy. He embodies lawlessness as revolt against divine authority. He is the son of destruction, marked by betrayal and destined for ruin. He exalts himself in the temple of God, usurping what belongs to Jehovah alone. He is a religious usurper rather than a merely secular tyrant. And he is destroyed by the appearing of Christ, whose sovereign Word and glorious coming end every false claim to divinity.

Chapter 9. The Restrainer and the Mystery of Lawlessness

The Mystery of Lawlessness Already at Work

Paul writes in 2 Thessalonians 2:6–8 with remarkable balance. On the one hand, the man of lawlessness had not yet been fully revealed. On the other hand, the principle that would culminate in that revelation was already active. This is why he says, "the mystery of lawlessness is already at work." That statement is one of the most important controls for the entire passage. It teaches the church that the final outbreak of lawless rebellion does not appear suddenly without prior development. It grows beneath the surface. It advances in concealed form before it emerges in unveiled form. The lawless one is revealed at the appointed time, but the lawless mystery was already operating in Paul's own day.

The word "mystery" here does not mean something irrational or unknowable. In apostolic usage, a mystery is a reality once hidden in full but now disclosed or made known by God's revelation. In this context, the "mystery of lawlessness" refers to a rebellious power already active in history, though not yet fully exposed in its mature public form. The church therefore must not think only in terms of abrupt end-time drama. Paul directs our attention to a deeper process. Lawlessness was not waiting idly in the future. It was already present as a working force in the apostolic age. The seeds of revolt, false authority, religious corruption, and anti-God self-exaltation were already germinating while the apostles still ministered.

This harmonizes naturally with what John says in 1 John 2:18. John declares that the believers had heard antichrist was coming, and yet "even now many antichrists have arisen." The same pattern appears in both apostles. There is a future unveiling or concentrated expression, but there is also an already-present activity. John speaks of many antichrists and the spirit of antichrist already in the world. Paul speaks of the mystery of lawlessness already at work. These are not contradictory perspectives. They are complementary testimonies. Both insist that the church must recognize evil in its developing form, not merely wait for its final exposure.

This truth is crucial because it protects the church from two opposite errors. One error is to push all lawless rebellion into the future, as though nothing in Paul's own day could qualify as part of the process. Paul himself rejects that. The lawless mystery was already working. The other error is to deny any climactic manifestation because one sees only a general principle diffused across history. Paul rejects that as well. What was already working would one day be more openly revealed. The biblical view, therefore, is neither empty futurism nor flat reductionism. It is historical development moving toward appointed exposure.

The phrase "already at work" also shows that lawlessness is not merely social disorder or generalized sinfulness. Human sin has been active since the fall. Paul is speaking more specifically of a religious and institutional rebellion that develops within the sphere of profession and worship. The lawless mystery is tied to the apostasy and to the temple-setting described earlier in the chapter. It is not just wickedness in the broadest sense. It is anti-God self-exaltation gaining hidden traction in the professing sphere while not yet fully enthroned in public view. This explains why Paul's concern is not only ethical but ecclesial and theological. The church must watch for the quiet growth of rebellion where God's truth should be honored.

Acts 20:29–31 provides a fitting parallel. Paul tells the Ephesian elders that after his departure savage wolves will enter among them, not sparing the flock, and that from among their own selves men will arise speaking twisted things to draw away disciples after them. That warning is essentially a description of the mystery of lawlessness at work beneath the surface. The wolves do not begin as fully exposed usurpers. The distorted speech begins within the visible sphere before the full consequences appear. Men arise, truth is twisted, disciples are drawn away, and only then does the corrupting process become more fully visible. Paul's warning to Thessalonica belongs to that same pattern. The lawless principle was already active, already corrupting, already pushing toward manifestation.

The church must therefore learn to recognize that the greatest threats are not always sudden. They may begin as tolerated distortion, growing ambition, institutional drift, and the slow enthronement of human authority over apostolic truth. By the time the lawless one is openly revealed, the underlying mystery has already been at work for some time. That is why spiritual watchfulness must begin before the final stage. The faithful must not ask only, "Has the climactic form appeared?" They must also ask, "Is the lawless principle already operating where Christ's authority should reign?" Paul's answer for his own day was yes. That answer gives the church a sober framework for every generation.

What Was Holding Back Full Manifestation

Paul says to the Thessalonians, "you know what restrains him now, so that he will be revealed in his time," and then adds, "only he who now restrains will do so until he is out of the way" (2 Thessalonians 2:6–7). The basic point is clear even where interpretive humility is needed: the full manifestation of the lawless one was being held back in Paul's day. The mystery was already active, but the unveiling was not yet allowed to reach its appointed maturity. Restraint and operation existed side by side. Lawlessness was working, but it was not yet free to appear in its fullest public form.

The first duty in handling this passage is to stay close to what Paul actually emphasizes. He does not encourage the Thessalonians to indulge in speculative curiosity. He reminds them that they already know what restrains. This means the answer was tied to apostolic instruction they had previously received. The restraining reality was not meant to become an endless puzzle detached from the first-century context. Paul assumes that it made sense to those original hearers because he had taught them about it while present with them. Therefore, the safest way to proceed is not to survey every theory ever proposed, but to ask what best fits the apostolic setting, the flow of the passage, and the supporting texts.

In harmony with that context, the most coherent line is that apostolic presence and apostolic authority functioned as the restraint. The apostles, appointed directly by Christ and bearing foundational authority in the church, stood as a living barrier against the full public development of lawless usurpation. Their teaching preserved the churches in sound doctrine. Their personal ministry exposed falsehood. Their inspired authority prevented rebellion from maturing without challenge. The mystery of lawlessness was already operating, but while the apostolic witness still stood in living force, the full revelation of the lawless one was held back.

This reading fits the logic of Paul's words. The restraint is not necessarily one narrow mechanical force. It is a restraining reality operating through the apostolic era. Paul can speak of "what restrains" and "he who now restrains" because the restraint includes both the objective apostolic ministry and the living apostolic presence through which that ministry is exercised. The ministry, doctrine, office, and personal witness stand together. The apostles were not merely individual pious men. They were Christ-appointed bearers of foundational truth and discipline within the church. Through them, lawless ambition could not yet seize the sphere of profession in its mature public form.

Ephesians 2:20 strengthens this understanding by saying that the household of God has been built on the foundation of the apostles and prophets, Christ Jesus Himself being the cornerstone. A foundation has a preserving and ordering function. It establishes the true form of the house. As long as the apostolic foundation was being actively laid and guarded through living apostolic ministry, the church possessed a divinely appointed restraint against the enthronement of counterfeit authority. Lawlessness could work in hidden ways, but it could not yet fully occupy the house while the foundational witnesses of Christ still stood in active office.

This also fits the pastoral tone of 2 Thessalonians. Paul is not giving the church a cryptic code for later generations to decode in isolation. He is reassuring a troubled congregation that the lawless rebellion has not already reached its climactic unveiling. Why not? Because the restraining order established in their own time had not yet been removed. The apostolic structure was still in place. The mystery was real, but the appointed barrier had not yet given way. The Thessalonians therefore had no reason to conclude that the day of the Lord had already arrived.

The Apostolic Era as a Restraining Force

The New Testament repeatedly presents the apostolic era as uniquely stabilizing for the church. This does not mean the apostles eliminated all falsehood from the churches. Clearly they did not. But it does mean their presence, authority, and ongoing ministry held back the full emergence of organized lawless usurpation. Acts 20:29–31 is especially revealing. Paul does not tell the Ephesian elders that the wolves had already fully triumphed. He says, "after my departure" fierce wolves will come in among you. He also says that from among their own selves men will arise, speaking twisted things to draw away disciples after them. The implication is plain. Paul's own presence and active ministry had a restraining effect. The danger existed already, but his departure would open the way for a deeper outbreak.

The same pattern appears in 2 Timothy 4:6–8. Paul says, "the time of my departure has come." He knows his earthly course is nearly finished. That statement should not be detached from the broader apostolic concern about preserving sound doctrine after the apostles' deaths. Paul had fought the good fight, finished the course, and kept the faith. Yet the very fact that he speaks this way underscores the transitional moment. A living apostolic witness was passing from the scene. The church would continue to possess apostolic Scripture and apostolic truth, but the personal restraining presence of Christ's appointed foundational witnesses would no longer stand in the same way against the growth of lawless corruption.

Second Peter 1:12–15 contributes to the same picture. Peter says he will continue to remind the believers of the truth they know, and he recognizes that the putting off of his earthly dwelling is near. He is careful that after his departure they will be able to recall these things. Again the pattern is striking. The apostle knows he will soon die. He therefore labors to preserve the truth in written and remembered form because his living voice will soon be removed. This is not accidental in relation to the doctrine of restraint. If apostolic presence functioned as a barrier against full lawless manifestation, then apostolic departure would necessarily mark the transition from stronger restraint to greater vulnerability.

This line also agrees with 1 John 2:18. John says, "it is the last hour," and that many antichrists had already arisen. Yet he writes as an aged apostle still warning, exposing, and correcting. The antichristic principle was active while at least one apostle still lived, but John's own ministry served to identify and oppose it. In that sense the apostolic era was a time of simultaneous operation and restraint. The danger was already real, but it had not yet reached its full historical maturity. Apostolic authority still confronted the deceivers directly.

This should not be misunderstood as though the restraining force were merely human personality. The apostles restrained lawlessness because Christ appointed them, equipped them, and spoke through them. Their authority was ministerial and foundational, not self-generated. What restrained was not human greatness in itself, but the divinely instituted apostolic order in the church. That is why Ephesians 2:20 matters so much. The apostles and prophets are foundational because Christ chose them to establish His house in truth. When that unique era passed, the church remained bound to their inspired teaching, but the living foundational presence that had checked lawless usurpation in a distinct way was gone.

This interpretation also preserves the historical concreteness of Paul's words. He tells the Thessalonians that they know what restrains. That suggests something intelligible in their own setting, not a far-removed theory requiring later speculation. They knew Paul. They had received his instruction. They lived within the apostolic age. They could understand that the full unveiling had not yet come because the divinely appointed apostolic order was still operative. This keeps the chapter anchored in the first-century context and avoids transforming the restrainer into an abstraction with no relation to the church Paul was actually writing to.

From Restraint to Exposure

Paul says the restraining action continues "until he is out of the way," and then "the lawless one will be revealed" (2 Thessalonians 2:7–8). The movement is therefore from restraint to exposure. That transition must be understood historically and theologically. The lawless principle is already operative, but its public enthronement is delayed until the restraining force no longer holds it back in the same manner. Once that restraint is removed from the scene, what had been working in hidden fashion moves toward clearer historical manifestation.

This does not mean that the moment of transition can be reduced to one simplistic date or one mechanical event. Paul's own wording points to an ordered shift rather than a theatrical instant comprehensible apart from the larger historical process. The restraint remains for a time; then it no longer functions in the same way; then the lawless one is revealed in his own appointed season. This fits well with the apostolic-presence view. As the apostles finished their course and passed from the scene, the church entered a period in which the mystery of lawlessness could advance with fewer living barriers. The written apostolic deposit remained fully authoritative, but the direct foundational governance and correction of the apostles themselves no longer stood in the midst of the churches.

Acts 20 again provides a striking parallel. Paul warns the elders while he is still present, then speaks of what will happen after his departure. That is the movement from restraint to greater exposure. The wolves are not absent before his departure in an absolute sense, but they are kept from fuller activity by the active oversight of apostolic authority. Once that oversight is removed, the hidden danger advances more openly. The same dynamic appears in the Thessalonian passage. Lawlessness is already there, but not yet fully unveiled. The restraining order still stands. When that order passes, the exposure becomes more public.

This also explains why Paul's teaching should not lead the church into panic whenever it sees corruption grow. The movement from restraint to exposure is governed by divine appointment. The lawless one is revealed "in his time." That phrase is crucial. The unveiling is not merely the triumph of evil ingenuity. It occurs only at the appointed time under God's sovereignty. The same Lord who established the restraint also determines when the restraint gives way and when exposure occurs. Therefore, the church should never imagine that history is simply running loose. Even the progression from hidden lawlessness to public revelation unfolds under divine timing.

The phrase "out of the way" should likewise be read with sobriety. It does not require the church to speculate wildly about violent removal, supernatural disappearance, or every dramatic theory that later imagination has proposed. The basic point is enough for Paul's argument: the restraining reality ceases to function in the same active manner, and then the lawless unveiling advances. In light of the apostolic-supporting texts, the most coherent understanding is that the apostolic era passed, the living foundational witnesses completed their ministry, and the church moved into a new phase of history in which concealed lawlessness could ripen toward institutional and public expression.

This transition is sobering, but it is not hopeless. The removal of living apostolic presence did not leave the church without the Word of God. The apostolic Scriptures remained, and they remain. What changed was the direct historical restraint exercised through the apostles' continuing earthly ministry. Thus the chapter should not be read as though once the apostles died the church was abandoned. Rather, the point is that a distinct restraining phase in redemptive history gave way to a phase of greater exposure, precisely as Paul warned. The faithful response is therefore not despair, but deeper submission to the apostolic Word that still stands as the church's infallible rule.

Why the Revealing of the Lawless One Is Historical and Progressive

One of the most important conclusions to draw from 2 Thessalonians 2:6–8 is that the revealing of the lawless one is both historical and progressive. It is historical because Paul roots the process in the church's actual movement through time. The mystery was already at work in his day. The restraint was active in his day. The unveiling would occur in its appointed time. This is not abstract timeless symbolism detached from history. It is the outworking of rebellion within the visible sphere of the church across real historical development. The lawless one is not dropped into the world without preparation. He emerges through a process Paul says had already begun.

It is progressive because Paul distinguishes between hidden operation and public revelation. The mystery is active first; the unveiling comes later. This means the church must think in terms of growth, ripening, and exposure. Lawlessness advances by stages. It begins in covert distortion, ambition, and revolt against apostolic truth. It matures through increasing corruption and self-exaltation. It reaches a point where what was once beneath the surface becomes publicly manifest in concentrated form. This pattern keeps the reader from shallow interpretation. One must not expect the climactic form to appear without antecedents, nor dismiss the antecedents because they do not yet look fully developed.

This progressive dimension also helps explain why the lawless one can be spoken of both as future and as somehow already present in principle. The same is true in John's teaching about antichrist. John says antichrist is coming, and yet many antichrists have already arisen. Paul says the lawless one will be revealed, and yet the mystery of lawlessness is already at work. In both cases, the biblical model is historical progression toward concentration. The future form is real, but it grows out of a present reality already active in seed and structure.

Such an approach also guards against date-fixing sensationalism. If the revealing is historical and progressive, then it should not be treated as though every frightening moment instantly exhausts the prophecy. Nor should the church ignore the long maturation of revolt while waiting for one dramatic sign. The faithful must instead watch how apostolic truth is treated, how human authority exalts itself in the sphere of worship, how corruption deepens beneath outward profession, and how the hidden principle of lawlessness moves toward more open manifestation. This is a more biblical form of watchfulness than mere excitement over current events.

The historical-progressive reading further preserves the church's task in every age. Believers are not called simply to identify the final stage when it arrives. They are called to oppose the mystery of lawlessness at every stage by clinging to apostolic doctrine, refusing corrupt authority, and testing all claims in the light of Christ's Word. If lawlessness matures historically, then resistance to it must also be historically constant. Every generation must guard against the hidden beginnings of what later becomes open usurpation. The church loses much when it waits only for the end while tolerating the principle in the present.

Therefore the revealing of the lawless one should be understood as the exposure of a rebellion already developing in the apostolic era, held back for a time by the restraining force of apostolic presence and authority, and then moving progressively toward clearer manifestation once that foundational restraining era passed. This reading remains close to Paul's text, fits the supporting passages, and avoids unhelpful speculation. It honors the first-century setting, preserves the continuity between hidden mystery and revealed lawlessness, and shows why the church must always measure religious claims by the apostolic foundation laid once for all in Christ.

Paul's teaching in this section is thus both sobering and stabilizing. The mystery of lawlessness was already at work. Something was holding back its full manifestation. The apostolic era itself functioned as a restraining force. From that restraint history would move toward greater exposure. And the revealing of the lawless one would be real, progressive, and governed by divine timing. The church is therefore taught neither to panic nor to daydream, but to understand the historical development of apostate rebellion under the sovereign hand of God and to remain steadfast in the apostolic truth that alone exposes every counterfeit authority.

Chapter 10. Lying Signs, Judicial Delusion, and the Doom of the Lawless One

The Satanic Energy Behind Lawlessness

Paul declares in 2 Thessalonians 2:9 that the coming of the lawless one is "according to the working of Satan." That statement takes the discussion beyond mere institutional corruption or human religious ambition. The lawless one is certainly connected to apostasy, false authority, and self-exaltation in the sphere of worship, but Paul now uncovers the deeper source empowering that rebellion. Behind the lawless order stands Satan himself. This does not mean the lawless one ceases to be historically real, morally guilty, or fully responsible. It does mean that the rebellion is not merely sociological or psychological. It is spiritual warfare brought into public expression. Satan energizes the lawless order because the lawless order is one of his chief instruments for opposing Christ, corrupting the truth, and ensnaring those who do not love the gospel.

This is entirely in harmony with the broader biblical witness. Jesus says in John 8:44 that the Devil "was a murderer from the beginning" and "does not stand in the truth, because truth is not in him." He is a liar and the father of the lie. That description helps explain why Paul links Satan's working with deception, false signs, and destructive judgment. Satan does not merely attack through crude persecution. He also attacks through counterfeit religion, persuasive fraud, and doctrinal distortion. His aim is not only to intimidate; it is to deceive. He seeks to occupy the sphere of worship with falsehood so that men may be alienated from God while imagining themselves spiritually secure.

This is why Paul's language must not be weakened. He does not say only that the lawless one happens to use deceptive methods. He says the lawless one comes "according to the working of Satan." The word points to operative energy, effective activity, and purposeful influence. Satan is not a passive observer of apostasy. He is its great enemy-source, the one who drives counterfeit religion toward its mature form. Wherever the truth of Christ is displaced by exalted human authority, false worship, or lying wonders, the satanic character of the movement must be recognized. The rebellion is not merely against the church. It is against Jehovah, His Christ, and His saving truth.

At the same time, Paul's wording does not grant Satan independence from divine rule. Satan works, but he works under limit and under sentence. Just as the lawless one is ultimately destroyed by the appearance of Christ's coming, so the satanic energy behind him is neither sovereign nor permanent. This is pastorally important. The church must see the seriousness of demonic deception without falling into fear-driven exaggeration. Satan is powerful, but he is not God. He can deceive, but he cannot overturn Jehovah's purpose. He can energize false religion, but he cannot preserve it from final judgment. The Lord Jesus Christ remains the One before whom every lying power collapses.

This verse also helps explain why mere human analysis is never enough when dealing with apostasy. A church may identify organizational corruption, intellectual error, and moral compromise, and those things matter. Yet if it stops there, it will not grasp the full seriousness of the matter. Paul says there is a satanic working behind the lawless order. Therefore, the church must respond not only with institutional reform or theological clarity, but with spiritual vigilance, steadfast devotion to the truth, and utter dependence upon God's revealed Word. Satanic deception is not overcome by cleverness alone. It is overcome by faithfulness to Christ, love for the truth, and refusal to receive anything that contradicts the apostolic gospel.

Lying Signs and Wonders

Paul continues by saying that the lawless one comes "with all power and signs and lying wonders" (2 Thessalonians 2:9). This is one of the most sobering statements in the chapter because it shows that deception may appear clothed in impressive displays. Error does not always come looking weak, foolish, or easily dismissed. It may appear persuasive. It may seem powerful. It may bear the marks of supernatural impressiveness. Yet Paul calls these wonders what they truly are: lying wonders. Their purpose is not to authenticate divine truth but to serve falsehood. Their appearance of power does not make them holy. Their impressiveness does not make them true. Their effect is to strengthen deception, not to confirm the gospel.

This principle was already established in Deuteronomy 13:1–5. Moses warned Israel that if a prophet or dreamer arose and gave a sign or wonder, and the sign or wonder came true, but then said, "Let us go after other gods," the people must not listen to him. That passage is essential because it proves that miraculous appearance is never the final test of truth. Jehovah allows His people to be tested by whether they love Him with all their heart and soul. The decisive issue is not whether something extraordinary occurs, but whether the message leads men into fidelity to God or away from Him. A sign severed from truth becomes an instrument of seduction. Deuteronomy therefore lays down a principle Paul carries forward: counterfeit wonders may have persuasive force, but they must be judged by the revealed Word of God.

Jesus gives the same warning in Matthew 24:24. False christs and false prophets will arise and perform great signs and wonders to mislead, if possible, even the chosen ones. Once again, the church is told in advance that external impressiveness is no guarantee of divine approval. The religious world is often vulnerable at precisely this point. Men love the dramatic. They are fascinated by spectacle. They are eager for visible proofs, urgent manifestations, and extraordinary claims. Yet Christ warns that great signs may accompany great deception. What determines truth is not outward force but conformity to the message He has already given.

Paul's phrase "all power and signs and lying wonders" suggests the breadth of the counterfeit. The lawless order does not rely on one trick only. It presents a whole theater of persuasive power. "Power" emphasizes the impression of mighty activity. "Signs" suggests meaningful displays that claim to point beyond themselves. "Wonders" stresses the effect of astonishment upon those who see them. Yet all of it is organized in the service of falsehood. They are "lying" wonders because they are attached to the lie. Their whole function is to make falsehood look glorious, credible, and spiritually irresistible.

This should awaken the church to a permanent danger. Many religious movements gain influence not by careful exposition of Scripture but by displays that produce amazement, urgency, and emotional submission. Men become convinced not because truth has conquered the conscience, but because spectacle has captured the imagination. Paul warns that such things can belong to the sphere of the lawless one. The believer must therefore test every claim, every sign, every wonder, and every assertion of spiritual power by the apostolic doctrine of Christ. A wonder that leads away from truth is not sanctified by its effect. It is condemned by its purpose.

Revelation 13:13–15 provides a striking parallel. The second beast performs great signs, even making fire come down from heaven, and by those signs deceives those who dwell on the earth. That text will be treated more fully in the next chapter, but it should be noted here because it confirms Paul's basic point. Satanic deception often operates through counterfeit signs tied to worship corruption. The signs are not ends in themselves. They are instruments leading men into false allegiance. That is why the church must never treat the miraculous in isolation from doctrine. The question is not simply whether something astonishing occurred. The question is what truth the event serves, what allegiance it demands, and whether it honors Jehovah and His Christ according to Scripture.

Why Deception Captures the Truth-Rejecting

Paul next explains why this deception succeeds. It comes "with every wicked deception for those who are perishing, because they did not accept the love of the truth so as to be saved" (2 Thessalonians 2:10). This is one of the most searching statements in the chapter because it reveals that the success of deception is not finally due to intellectual brilliance on the side of the deceiver. It is due to moral refusal on the side of the deceived. Men are captured by the lie because they do not love the truth. They may hear it, examine it outwardly, discuss it, and even use some of its language, but they do not welcome it with a heart that treasures it as life from God.

The wording is exact. Paul does not say merely that they failed to understand the truth. He says they did not receive "the love of the truth." The issue is deeper than bare cognition. It is affection, allegiance, and moral response. Truth in Scripture is not a neutral set of propositions waiting to be filed away. It is the saving revelation of God in Christ. To love the truth is to embrace it as good, righteous, life-giving, and authoritative. To refuse that love is to remain exposed to deception even if one possesses impressive religious knowledge. Men are not saved by intellectual contact with truth alone. They are saved as the truth is received, loved, and held fast in faith.

This explains why falsehood can have such power over outwardly religious people. They may admire religious structure, enjoy spiritual excitement, and hunger for signs, but if they do not love the truth of Christ, they are vulnerable to the lie. Deception succeeds where the conscience has already set itself against God's Word. The lie offers what the unconverted heart wants: religion without submission, spirituality without repentance, power without holiness, authority without truth, and worship redirected toward what man can control. That is why Paul says the deception is "wicked." It fits a wicked desire. It is welcomed because it flatters rebellion.

Romans 1:18–25 throws powerful light on this process. Paul says men suppress the truth in unrighteousness. Though they know God at the level of general revelation, they do not honor Him as God or give thanks. They become futile in their reasonings, their foolish heart is darkened, and they exchange the truth of God for the lie. That exchange is the deep root of all judicial deception. Men do not arrive at the lie by innocent misfortune. They trade truth for what suits their rebellion. They exchange worship of the Creator for worship of the creature. That same pattern stands behind 2 Thessalonians 2. Those who perish do so because they refuse the truth that would save them and embrace the falsehood that destroys them.

This means the church must be very clear about the moral dimension of doctrinal error. The lie is not merely an unfortunate conclusion reached through defective reasoning. It is often the chosen refuge of a heart unwilling to submit to God. To love the truth is to submit to Christ as He is revealed in Scripture. To reject that truth is to open the soul to increasing deception. This is why the great battle in apostasy is not only over information. It is over love. What do men love more than the truth? What are they willing to embrace instead of it? Whose authority do they really want over them?

The phrase "those who are perishing" also deserves attention. Paul is not describing neutral seekers caught in tragic confusion. He is describing persons on the path of destruction because they refuse the only truth that saves. Their perishing is not arbitrary. It is the moral outcome of rejecting God's revelation. That is why the lawless order can captivate them. The lie finds ready soil in hearts already estranged from the truth. A church that understands this will not place its confidence in clever strategies alone. It will pray and labor for hearts transformed by God so that men may not merely hear the truth, but love it.

God's Judicial Handing Over

Paul then states something even more solemn: "For this reason God sends upon them a working of delusion so that they may believe the lie, in order that they all may be judged who did not believe the truth but took pleasure in unrighteousness" (2 Thessalonians 2:11–12). This is not easy language, but it is holy and necessary language. It reveals that divine judgment may take the form of handing men over to the deception they have chosen. God is never the author of evil, never the father of lies, and never morally implicated in satanic falsehood. Yet in righteous judgment He may give over truth-rejecting men to the power of the lie as punishment for their refusal of the truth.

Romans 1 again provides a close parallel. Because men exchange the truth of God for the lie and refuse to honor Him, "God gave them over" in the lusts of their hearts, to dishonorable passions, and to a debased mind. That handing over is both judgment and exposure. God gives men over to what they want apart from Him, and in doing so exposes the true corruption of their hearts. Second Thessalonians 2 works in the same way. The delusion does not fall upon those who humbly love the truth. It falls upon those who rejected the truth and delighted instead in unrighteousness. God's judicial action confirms them in the path they have chosen.

This judicial handing over must be understood in full moral clarity. Paul says it happens "for this reason." The reason is already given: they did not receive the love of the truth. Divine judgment is not arbitrary. It is righteous response to deliberate refusal. Men reject the gospel, prefer wickedness, and welcome deception. God then gives them over to the delusion that fits their rebellion. In that sense the judgment is terrible precisely because it is fitting. Those who did not want the truth are confirmed in falsehood. Those who would not believe are left to the lie. Those who took pleasure in unrighteousness are given a judgment consistent with that pleasure.

This also reveals why doctrinal rebellion is never harmless. When men habitually resist truth, they do not remain spiritually stationary. Refusal hardens. Suppression darkens. Rebellion invites judgment. One of the forms of that judgment is increased inability to perceive and receive what is true. The conscience becomes more seared. The appetite for deception grows. What once might have seemed outrageous becomes plausible, then attractive, then binding. That is divine judgment operating through moral consequence under God's sovereign hand.

At the same time, this passage should drive the church to holy fear and gratitude. Fear, because it reveals the seriousness of rejecting the gospel. Gratitude, because any love for the truth found in believers is the fruit of divine mercy, not human superiority. No Christian should read 2 Thessalonians 2:11–12 with pride, as though he naturally escaped deception by his own virtue. The proper response is humility before God, deepened love for the truth, and earnest prayer that Jehovah would preserve His people from the lie.

This text also teaches the church not to measure divine judgment only by outward catastrophe. Sometimes judgment falls as blindness. Sometimes it falls as spiritual enslavement. Sometimes it appears as confidence in falsehood. A man may feel religiously certain while standing under divine delusion. That is a terrifying reality. It means the absence of outward suffering is no proof of divine favor. A community may flourish outwardly, display power, and attract admiration, while actually standing under God's judicial handing over because it has rejected the truth. That is why discernment must be tied to Scripture rather than to visible success.

The Certain Judgment of the Lawless Order

Paul's final purpose clause in this section is unmistakable: "in order that they all may be judged who did not believe the truth but took pleasure in unrighteousness" (2 Thessalonians 2:12). The lawless order is not merely exposed as false. It is destined for judgment. Those who embrace the lie are not merely mistaken. They are condemned because they preferred unrighteousness to truth. This brings the chapter to its necessary moral end. Satanic deception, counterfeit power, lying wonders, and judicial delusion all move toward one fixed outcome: divine judgment.

The certainty of this judgment is already woven through the whole context. The lawless one is destroyed by the appearance of Christ's coming in 2 Thessalonians 2:8. Here Paul widens the lens to include those who follow the lie. The leader and the led alike stand under the sentence of God when they reject the truth. This does not erase differences of role or degree of guilt, but it does show that participation in the lawless order is not spiritually neutral. To join oneself to the lie is to stand in opposition to God. To refuse the truth of Christ is to remain under wrath.

The basis of judgment is also carefully stated. Paul does not say they are judged because truth was unavailable. He says they are judged because they "did not believe the truth" and "took pleasure in unrighteousness." There is both negative refusal and positive delight. They reject what is true and embrace what is evil. This is why the lawless order is so grave. It is not simply error of mind. It is corruption of desire. Men love what destroys them. They enjoy the very unrighteousness that prepares their judgment. The lie suits them because it protects their pleasures from the claims of God.

This judgment theme should also shape how the church views false religion. False religion is often praised by the world so long as it is impressive, inclusive of error, and detached from the exclusive truth of Christ. Yet Scripture says its end is not honor but condemnation. No lying wonder will survive Christ's appearing. No counterfeit authority will escape His judgment. No delusion will remain once the truth stands openly before all creation. Therefore, the church must not envy the power of the lawless order, fear its outward displays, or measure by worldly standards what God has already condemned.

The parallel with Revelation 13:13–15 strengthens this point without requiring us to enter the full discussion reserved for the next chapter. There too signs are used to deceive, and the deception serves false worship. Paul and Revelation agree that counterfeit supernatural impressiveness is part of end-time rebellion, but both also assume divine judgment upon that rebellion. What appears astonishing to men remains detestable before God if it serves the lie. The church must never separate religious phenomena from their final moral verdict.

IDENTIFYING THE ANTICHRIST

What, then, is the church's duty in light of this chapter? It must cling to the truth and love it. It must not be dazzled by power detached from doctrine. It must test every claim by the revealed Word of God. It must understand that deception works through satanic energy, counterfeit signs, moral refusal of truth, and divine handing over of the rebellious. It must remember that judgment belongs not only to the lawless leader but to all who delight in the lie. And it must anchor its confidence in the certainty that Christ will not allow the lawless order to endure. The lie may flourish for a time, wonders may persuade many, and unrighteousness may be celebrated as wisdom, but the doom of the lawless order is fixed by the judgment of God and by the appearing of His Son.

In this way Paul's warning becomes both a theological unveiling and a pastoral safeguard. He shows the church how satanic deception works so that the church will not be naïve. He shows why the lie captivates so that believers will cultivate love for the truth. He reveals God's judicial handing over so that men will fear rejecting the gospel. And He declares the certain judgment of the lawless order so that the faithful will not lose heart. Every counterfeit power, every lying wonder, every cherished falsehood, and every pleasure in unrighteousness moves toward the same end: exposure before Jehovah and destruction under the reign of the Lord Jesus Christ.

Edward D. Andrews

Part Four: Revelation's Final Beastly Order

Chapter 11. The Beast From the Sea, the Beast From the Earth, and the Image of the Beast

The Dragon's War Continued in History

Revelation 13 does not begin a brand-new conflict. It continues the war already set forth in Revelation 12. There the dragon is identified as Satan, the serpent of old, the great adversary of God and His people. He is cast down, enraged, and determined to wage war against "the rest of her offspring, those who keep the commandments of God and hold to the testimony of Jesus" (Revelation 12:17). That statement is essential for understanding the entire chapter before us. Revelation 13 is not merely about strange beasts rising from sea and land in isolation from the broader narrative. It is about the dragon extending his war into history through visible agents and organized structures. Satan's hatred does not remain in the invisible realm. It takes shape in public institutions, coercive systems, false worship, and deceptive authority.

This means the beasts of Revelation 13 must be read as the dragon's historical instruments. The dragon himself is the unseen source of rebellion, but he does not ordinarily rule the nations in a naked and direct manner. He works through mediated forms of anti-God power. That is why the chapter moves from dragon to beast rather than from dragon directly to final judgment. The dragon gives the beast his power, his throne, and great authority. This line is decisive. The beast is not self-originating. Its energy, authority, and anti-God posture are dragonic in source, even though the beast is visibly historical and public in operation. The war of heaven's enemy now appears in earthly form.

This also helps us avoid two opposite errors. One error is to treat Revelation 13 as though it were about nothing more than individual spiritual temptation detached from political and institutional life. The other error is to reduce the beasts to mere civil powers without recognizing their satanic origin and religious function. John gives us neither reduction. He shows that the dragon's war enters the realm of empire, public authority, false worship, signs, and coercion. The conflict is therefore both spiritual and historical. It is spiritual in source and historical in manifestation. The anti-God order is not less than political, but it is more than political. It is organized rebellion against Jehovah expressed through structures of power and systems of allegiance.

Revelation 12:17 must remain in view because it tells us whom the dragon hates. He makes war on those who remain loyal to God and to Jesus Christ. Therefore the beasts of chapter 13 must also be understood in relation to the holy ones. They are not neutral institutions of public life. They are weapons in a war against the people of God. Their demand for worship, their use of deception, and their coercive measures all serve the dragon's larger purpose: to displace the worship of God, to silence the testimony of Jesus, and to draw the world into rebellious allegiance. Once this is understood, the chapter becomes far more coherent. The beasts are not random monsters. They are the dragon's historical strategy.

The same line appears again in Revelation 16:13, where unclean spirits like frogs come out of the mouth of the dragon, the beast, and the false prophet. That later text confirms that the dragon, beast, and false prophet belong to one anti-God coalition. The dragon is the satanic source, the beast is the public political expression of dragonic dominion, and the false prophet is the deceptive religious voice that supports and promotes beast-worship. Revelation 13 gives the church the first full portrait of this order. It shows how satanic hostility becomes institutional, how political power and religious deception are joined, and how idolatry becomes socially enforced. The chapter, therefore, is not merely about one isolated symbol. It is about the full anti-God order at work in history.

The Beast From the Sea as Daniel's Final Concentration

John says, "I saw a beast rising out of the sea, with ten horns and seven heads, with ten diadems on its horns and blasphemous names on its heads" (Revelation 13:1). This imagery immediately recalls Daniel 7, where the four great beasts arise from the sea. Daniel's sea is the restless realm of the nations, and from it emerge successive world powers marked by violence, arrogance, and hostility toward God. John's beast from the sea clearly stands in that prophetic stream. In fact, it is more than a mere repetition. It is Daniel's pattern brought to concentrated maturity. John's beast combines features of Daniel's leopard, bear, and lion, showing that the successive beastly empires of Daniel now converge into one final composite expression of rebellious dominion.

This is why the beast from the sea should be understood as the mature political expression of dragonic power. It is empire in its anti-God fullness. The state as ordained by God for justice is not the subject here. Revelation is not condemning civil order as such. Rather, it is unveiling political power once it has become beastly, blasphemous, and dragon-driven. The beast from the sea is public authority detached from submission to Jehovah and then energized by Satan to oppose His kingdom. That is why its heads bear blasphemous names. The issue is not mere administration. It is arrogant defiance of God expressed through public dominion.

The wound and apparent recovery in Revelation 13:3 heighten the impression of counterfeit majesty. One of the beast's heads appears as though slain to death, and yet its fatal wound is healed. The whole earth marvels and follows the beast. This does not present a true resurrection in the sense belonging to Christ. It presents a satanic parody, a counterfeit wonder that magnifies the beast in the eyes of the world. The effect is worshipful astonishment. Men do not merely acknowledge the beast's power politically. They are drawn into admiration, submission, and idolatrous allegiance. The beast is therefore not merely a government. It is government sacralized, government glorified, government demanding the kind of reverence that belongs only to God.

This is confirmed by Revelation 13:4: "they worshiped the dragon because he gave his authority to the beast, and they worshiped the beast, saying, 'Who is like the beast, and who can fight against it?'" Here the political character of the beast is inseparable from worship. The world does not simply obey it out of practical necessity. It marvels at it, reveres it, and through it worships the dragon. This is why the beast from the sea must not be reduced to a secular ruler alone. Its power is political, but its significance is religious. It becomes the focal point of idolatrous allegiance because dragonic power has been clothed in public sovereignty.

Revelation 17:3 and 17:8–14 strengthen this interpretation. There again John sees a beast, and the kings of the earth give their power and authority to it. The beast carries the broader anti-God order and gathers the rulers of the earth into one rebellious purpose. This is political concentration in open hostility to the Lamb. Yet even there the beast remains under divine limit and destined for destruction. Revelation 17 therefore helps us see the beast from the sea not as one disconnected ruler but as a mature political order, an organized concentration of anti-God dominion that gathers the kings of the earth into unified rebellion against Christ.

This Danielic background must not be lost. Daniel had already taught us to see empire as beastly when it exalts itself against God, persecutes the holy ones, and tramples truth. Revelation 13 shows the final concentration of that pattern. The beast from the sea is Daniel's beastly dominion ripened to its fullest anti-God form. It is the world-power principle reaching its dragonic maturity. It blasphemes, it persecutes, it demands worship, and it makes war on the holy ones. Yet like Daniel's beasts, it remains temporary. Its apparent greatness only magnifies the certainty of its downfall before the Lamb.

The Beast From the Earth as Deceptive Religious Power

John then sees "another beast rising out of the earth" (Revelation 13:11). If the first beast is the mature political expression of dragonic power, the second beast is the deceptive religious agent that serves and glorifies the first. This distinction is crucial for the whole chapter. The second beast is not identical with the first, though it serves the same anti-God order. Later in Revelation, this second beast is identified functionally as the false prophet. Its role is not primarily direct imperial conquest but spiritual seduction. It promotes worship of the first beast, performs signs, and persuades the inhabitants of the earth to submit to the beastly order.

The appearance of this second beast is especially striking. It has two horns like a lamb, yet it speaks like a dragon. That contrast is one of the most revealing images in the chapter. The beast from the earth presents itself in lamb-like form, suggesting religious mildness, spiritual legitimacy, or a counterfeit likeness to Christ. Yet its voice gives it away. It speaks as the dragon speaks. Outwardly it imitates innocence; inwardly and verbally it serves satanic rebellion. This is the very essence of deceptive religious power. It does not normally arrive looking openly monstrous. It comes with lamb-like appearance, spiritual claims, religious language, and a semblance of legitimacy, all while speaking for the dragon.

Its entire ministry is directed toward the exaltation of the first beast. Revelation 13:12 says it exercises all the authority of the first beast in its presence and makes the earth and its inhabitants worship the first beast, whose mortal wound was healed. That line is decisive.

The second beast is not an independent spiritual movement. It is the religious arm of the anti-God political order. It exists to produce worshipful allegiance to beastly power. It sacralizes the political order. It interprets beast-power as worthy of reverence. It teaches the world to bow.

This is why the second beast must be understood as deceptive religious power rather than mere civil propaganda in a narrow sense. Its signs, its voice, and its worship-directing function all place it in the sphere of religion. Revelation 13:13–14 says it performs great signs and deceives those who dwell on the earth. This language aligns directly with the biblical pattern of false prophets, lying wonders, and satanic deception already discussed in earlier chapters. The second beast is Revelation's great symbolic portrait of false religion serving anti-God dominion. It does not merely bless political order in a neutral way. It baptizes rebellion with sacred significance.

Revelation 19:20 confirms this identification when it says that the beast was captured, "and with it the false prophet who in its presence had done the signs by which he deceived those who had received the mark of the beast and those who worshiped its image." The second beast, then, is the false prophet in symbolic form. It is not primarily military in nature, though it supports coercive power. It is primarily deceptive and cultic. It operates in the realm of sign, persuasion, worship, and false certification of anti-God authority. This is why it is so dangerous. Political power can command submission externally, but deceptive religion can capture the conscience, shape imagination, and direct worship.

The church must therefore recognize that Revelation's anti-God order is never merely political. Beastly dominion is sustained and magnified by false spiritual power. The second beast teaches the world how to adore the first. It transforms public rebellion into sacred duty. It persuades men that submission to the beast is not merely prudent but proper. This is one of the most serious forms of satanic deception in Scripture: religion not merely corrupted, but weaponized in service of dragonic dominion.

The Image of the Beast as Institutionalized Idolatry

The next development in the chapter is the making of the image of the beast. Revelation 13:14–15 says that the earth-dwellers are told to make an image for the beast, and the second beast is permitted to give breath to the image so that it even speaks and causes those who will not worship it to be killed. The image of the beast must be understood as the institutionalized form of the idolatrous order. It is not merely one more symbol added at random. It is the visible and organized embodiment of beast-worship. The beastly system now has a cultic form by which allegiance is displayed, enforced, and made public.

This image concept stands firmly in the biblical pattern of idolatry. In Scripture, an image is never a harmless artistic object when connected to worship. It is the visible representation of false devotion, the attempt to give concrete form to rebellious reverence. Here in Revelation, the image is more than personal superstition. It is socially constructed and publicly authorized. Men are told to make it. It is then animated in a counterfeit manner and used to compel worship. This is why the image should be seen as institutionalized idolatry. The anti-God order does not stop with inward admiration for the beast. It builds structures, symbols, forms, and demands through which beast-worship becomes organized and enforceable.

This also explains why the image belongs so closely with the second beast. The false religious power does not merely preach reverence for the political order; it creates the cultic machinery by which that reverence becomes normalized and compulsory. It fashions a visible order of worship around beast-power. The image is therefore not simply a statue in the narrowest sense, though the symbolism may include that idea. It is the institutional form of beastly idolatry, the apparatus by which anti-God dominion becomes publicly honored and religiously enforced.

The language of giving "breath" to the image is especially revealing. This is not true creation, because creation belongs to God alone. It is counterfeit animation, a satanic parody of life that lends persuasive force to the idolatrous order. Once again Revelation shows that evil does not merely oppose the truth openly; it imitates, counterfeits, and mimics sacred realities. The beastly system has its political head, its religious prophet, and now its cultic image. It becomes a full anti-God order with power, proclamation, and worship-form all working together.

The coercive dimension is equally important. The image "causes" those who refuse worship to be killed. Thus idolatry and persecution are joined. The image is not decorative; it is judicial and disciplinary. It becomes an instrument of death against those who remain faithful to God. This shows that the image is part of the institutional machinery of anti-God society. It represents a social order in which false worship is not optional but demanded, and refusal is treated as a punishable offense. This is why the image belongs to the broader beastly system rather than existing as an isolated religious symbol. It is an enforced expression of allegiance to the anti-God order.

This development also deepens the contrast between the holy ones and the earth-dwellers. The world accepts the image because it has already marveled at the beast and embraced the dragon's order. The faithful refuse because they know that worship belongs to Jehovah alone. Therefore the image becomes a dividing point. It reveals where allegiance truly lies. It institutionalizes idolatry, but in doing so it also exposes those who will not bow. Revelation's purpose is not to fascinate us with religious machinery. It is to show how anti-God power reaches a stage where political dominion, deceptive religion, and idolatrous institution all stand together against the worship of the true God.

Why Revelation Presents a Political-Religious Composite

When the beast from the sea, the beast from the earth, and the image of the beast are taken together, Revelation presents a political-religious composite, not a single flat symbol doing every kind of work at once. This distinction is necessary if the chapter is to remain clear. The first beast is the mature political expression of dragonic power.

IDENTIFYING THE ANTICHRIST

The second beast is the deceptive religious agent that promotes and enforces worship of the first. The image is the institutionalized form of that idolatrous order. The three belong together, but they are not identical. Each serves a distinct function within the anti-God system.

This composite structure reflects how rebellion actually operates in history. Political power alone does not secure total allegiance. It needs religious legitimation. Religious deception alone does not dominate the world in full public force. It seeks alliance with institutional power. Idolatrous forms do not arise in a vacuum. They are crafted to embody and enforce the worship demanded by the broader system. Revelation, therefore, is not describing scattered evils without relation. It is unveiling a coherent anti-God order in which Satan works through political sovereignty, deceptive prophecy, and cultic institution to oppose God and persecute His people.

This also explains why Revelation 17:12–14 and Revelation 19:19–20 speak in terms of alliance and shared doom. The kings of the earth unite with the beast. The false prophet works in the beast's presence. The beast and false prophet are captured together. These later texts confirm what chapter 13 already shows: the anti-God order is composite and coordinated. It is not one bare office, one individual personality, or one mere idea. It is an organized system of rebellion bringing together dominion, deception, and worship corruption under the dragon's influence.

Such a reading is also faithful to the larger biblical pattern. Daniel had already shown beastly empire and blasphemous rulers. Jesus had already warned of false christs, false prophets, and desecrating intrusion into the holy sphere. Paul had already described apostasy, lawlessness, and lying wonders. Revelation 13 does not contradict those earlier passages. It gathers them into one symbolic portrait. The beast from the sea corresponds to beastly dominion in its final anti-God maturity. The beast from the earth corresponds to deceptive religious power and false prophetic activity. The image corresponds to the institutionalized idolatry by which false allegiance becomes visible and coercive. The chapter therefore stands as a grand synthesis of biblical prophecy concerning organized rebellion against God.

This composite reading also prevents a common mistake: collapsing all anti-God figures into one undifferentiated enemy. Scripture is more precise than that. The dragon is not the beast. The beast from the sea is not the beast from the earth. The image is not identical with either beast. Yet all of them work together. Such precision matters because it allows later chapters to treat the mark and the number with proper clarity. The mark belongs to this system of enforced allegiance. The number belongs to the beast's name and identity within this system. But those features should not be rushed here. The order itself must first be clearly seen.

Revelation 13, then, presents the church with the full anti-God order in symbolic form. Satan wages war through history by empowering beastly political dominion. That dominion is exalted and interpreted by deceptive religious power. That false religious power then gives institutional form to idolatry through the image of the beast and uses coercion to enforce worship. The result is a world-order demanding allegiance in direct opposition to Jehovah and to His Christ. The holy ones stand in sharp contrast to this order precisely because they refuse to worship what the world adores.

This prepares the way for the next stage of the prophecy. Once the political-religious composite is in place, the question naturally becomes: how does this order identify its own, enforce participation, and mark allegiance? Revelation answers that question by speaking of the mark of the beast. And once the mark is introduced, another question follows: what is the meaning of the beast's number, 666? Those matters belong to the chapters that follow. For now, the foundation has been laid. The beast from the sea, the beast from the earth, and the image of the beast together reveal the mature anti-God order through which the dragon wages war in history, demands worship, persecutes the faithful, and prepares the world for the final exposure of its rebellion before the victorious return of Jesus Christ.

Chapter 12. The Mark of the Beast: Worship, Allegiance, and Economic Submission

Forehead and Hand in Biblical Symbolism

The mark of the beast cannot be understood correctly unless it is read in light of the Bible's own symbolism concerning the forehead and the hand. Revelation 13:16–17 says that the beastly order "causes all, the small and the great, and the rich and the poor, and the free and the slave, to be given a mark on their right hand or on their forehead." Many readers immediately rush past the biblical background and treat the language as though it must first describe a modern technological object. But John does not write into a vacuum. Scripture had already established the symbolic force of these bodily locations long before Revelation was given. The forehead signifies what openly identifies a person, especially in thought, confession, loyalty, and conscious devotion. The hand signifies action, labor, service, and practical obedience. Together they point to the totality of allegiance: what a person inwardly embraces and outwardly performs.

This background is already present in the Law. Exodus 13:9 speaks of Jehovah's deliverance from Egypt being "as a sign on your hand and as a memorial between your eyes." Verse 16 repeats the same pattern. Deuteronomy 6:6–8 likewise commands that Jehovah's words be on the heart, tied as a sign on the hand, and as frontlets between the eyes. The point in those passages is not that Israel's covenant fidelity was reduced to a magical object. The point is that Jehovah's redeemed people were to be marked by His truth in thought and action. Their minds, their obedience, their daily conduct, and their public identity were all to be shaped by His covenant Word. The forehead and hand, therefore, already carry covenantal significance in Scripture. They signify belonging, remembrance, allegiance, and obedience.

That biblical pattern is indispensable for Revelation 13. John is not inventing strange body symbolism unrelated to the rest of Scripture. He is using already established covenant language and showing how the beastly order imitates and counterfeits what belongs to God. The mark on the forehead or hand is the beast's rival claim upon human beings. It signifies identification with the anti-God order in belief and behavior. The beast wants what Jehovah alone deserves: minds devoted to its falsehood and lives committed to its service. That is why the mark must not be treated as though its essential meaning were merely mechanical or commercial. The bodily imagery already tells the reader that the issue is deeper. It concerns the sphere of thought and the sphere of action, confession and conduct, inward loyalty and outward participation.

Ezekiel 9:4–6 confirms the same kind of symbolism from another angle. In that vision, those who groan over Jerusalem's abominations receive a mark on their foreheads, and they are distinguished from those under judgment. The forehead there clearly identifies a person in relation to divine evaluation. It marks out those who belong on one side of the dividing line rather than the other. Revelation later uses the same pattern with the servants of God sealed on their foreheads in

Revelation 7:3–4 and the Lamb's people bearing His name and the name of His Father on their foreheads in Revelation 14:1. Thus the mark of the beast belongs to a larger biblical contrast. Either one is marked out as belonging to God or marked out as belonging to the beastly order. The forehead and the hand are covenantally charged symbols of ownership, identity, and submission.

This is why Christians go astray when they begin the discussion with gadgets, commerce, or speculative identification instead of Scripture's own symbolic world. The first question is not, "What modern mechanism can this be matched to?" The first question is, "What does the Bible mean by forehead and hand?" Once that is answered, the theology of the mark becomes far clearer. The mark concerns public and practical solidarity with the anti-God system. It is not less than visible; Revelation presents it as real and consequential. But its reality is theological before it is technological. It marks out those whose thinking and doing have been claimed by the beast. In that sense the mark is the beast's counterfeit counterpart to Jehovah's covenant claim over His own people.

The Mark as Counter-Covenant Identity

Because the mark is rooted in biblical covenant symbolism, it must be understood as a counter-covenant identity. It is the beast's false seal, the beast's rival badge, the beast's claim upon those who belong to its order. Revelation 13 does not present the mark as an isolated detail. It appears only after the dragon, the beast from the sea, the beast from the earth, and the image of the beast have already been introduced. That sequence matters. The mark does not arise in a religious vacuum. It belongs to a fully developed anti-God system composed of dragonic power, beastly dominion, false prophetic deception, and institutionalized idolatry. The mark is the personal sign of attachment to that system. It is how the beastly order identifies its own.

This covenantal contrast becomes unmistakable when the primary and supporting texts are read together. Revelation 7:3–4 speaks of God's servants being sealed on their foreheads. Revelation 14:1 shows the Lamb standing on Mount Zion with the one hundred forty-four thousand, having His name and His Father's name written on their foreheads. Those texts establish the positive side of the symbolism. God marks His own. The Lamb's people bear His name. They are publicly and spiritually identified with Him. Revelation 13 presents the dark counterpart. The beast also marks people. It also claims identity. It also distinguishes those who belong to its order. The mark is therefore not a neutral identifier. It is a rival sign of ownership.

This is why the mark should be described as counter-covenant. It imitates covenant identity while directing allegiance away from Jehovah and the Lamb. In the covenant, God places His name upon His people. In the beastly parody, the beast places its mark upon its followers. In the covenant, God's people are to have His Word in mind and in practice. In the beastly counterfeit, the followers of the beast are marked in forehead and hand, that is, in thought and deed, as aligned with rebellion. In the covenant, God distinguishes and preserves His servants. In the beastly order, the followers of the beast are distinguished and organized under idolatrous authority. The mark is therefore a deeply theological reality. It is the anti-God order's answer to divine ownership.

Revelation 14:9–12 sharpens this with terrifying clarity. The third angel warns that if anyone worships the beast and its image and receives a mark on his forehead or on his hand, that person will drink the wine of the wrath of God. The connection is explicit. Worship of the beast, worship of its image, and receiving the mark belong together. John does not treat the mark as an unrelated civil convenience. He places it in the very context of idolatrous devotion. This means the mark is not simply an administrative label imposed on neutral people for practical reasons. It is bound up with participation in the beast's worshipful order. The one who receives it is not simply surviving in a hard economy. He is identifying with the anti-God system in a way Scripture treats as spiritually decisive.

That is why the language of "identity" is so important. The mark identifies a person with the beast just as the divine name identifies God's people with the Lamb and with the Father. Revelation 15:2 then speaks of those who had conquered the beast and its image and the number of its name. They stand beside the sea of glass, victorious because they did not yield allegiance to the beastly order. Revelation 20:4 adds that those who were faithful "had not worshiped the beast or its image and had not received the mark on their forehead and on their hand." Again the mark is inseparable from worship and allegiance. The faithful are distinguished precisely by refusing it. Their refusal is not a mere refusal of one outward token. It is refusal of the beast's claim over their identity.

This is also why the mark must not be trivialized into one narrow cultural fear detached from the covenantal structure of Revelation. The beast is after worship, submission, and social conformity. The mark expresses all three. It is the sign that one belongs to the anti-God order, accepts its claims, and acts accordingly. However the beastly system may manifest that demand in different historical forms, the theological meaning remains the same. The mark is the sign of covenantal treason, the beast's attempt to create a rival people bearing its own identifying sign rather than the name of God and the Lamb.

Why the Mark Is About Worship Before It Is About Commerce

One of the most persistent mistakes in handling the mark of the beast is to begin with commerce rather than worship. Revelation 13:17 does mention buying and selling, but Revelation itself places the mark first in the context of idolatrous allegiance. The order of the text matters. The beast from the earth causes the inhabitants of the earth to worship the first beast. It directs them to make an image for the beast. It enforces reverence toward that image. Only then does the mark appear in connection with economic restriction. This means the mark is about worship before it is about commerce. Commerce is the means of coercion, not the heart of the symbol.

Revelation 14:9–12 confirms this decisively. The angelic warning does not say, "If anyone participates in a commercial arrangement, he will suffer judgment." It says, "If anyone worships the beast and its image, and receives a mark on his forehead or on his hand," he will face the wrath of God. The mark is paired with worship because its deepest meaning is religious and covenantal. It is part of the beast's anti-God cultus. The issue is whom one acknowledges, whom one serves, and under whose authority one stands. To begin with technology, trade systems, or civil regulation while bypassing worship is to reverse Revelation's own emphasis.

This point is reinforced by Revelation 16:2, where the first bowl is poured out and harmful sores come upon the people who had the mark of the beast and worshiped its image. Once again the mark and beast-worship are joined. John does not separate them. The mark is not presented as though some innocent persons accidentally acquired it through ordinary social participation while remaining spiritually untouched. The marked are the worshipers. They belong to the anti-God order. They have accepted its identity and yielded to its demand. Revelation 19:20 says the false prophet deceived those who had received the mark of the beast and those who worshiped its image. The same intimate association appears again. The mark belongs to deception and worship, not to neutral economics.

This means the chapter must firmly reject the shallow theory that the mark is primarily a technological device detached from religious allegiance. That does not mean the beastly order cannot use visible mechanisms, public systems, economic controls, or social enforcement. Revelation plainly says it does. But those things are not the essence of the mark. The essence is allegiance expressed through thought and action within a system of false worship. A purely technological reading strips the mark of its biblical depth and reduces John's prophecy to one narrow kind of prediction. The text itself will not allow that. It places the mark within the sphere of beast-worship, image-veneration, false prophetic deception, and open hostility to those who belong to God.

That is why the mark can never be reduced to something as small as a piece of commerce by itself. Commerce matters because the beast uses it. But the issue is broader and deeper. The beastly order seeks to form a world in which worship, social belonging, and economic participation are joined under anti-God authority. The mark signifies willing conformity to that order. It is the sign that one accepts the beast's terms for public life and personal identity. Thus commerce becomes an instrument in a larger battle over worship.

The church must hold this distinction firmly because it affects pastoral faithfulness. If Christians are taught that the mark is only one future technological mechanism, they may fail to see the ongoing biblical principle: beastly powers always seek to attach social and economic pressure to false allegiance. The form may vary, but the theological substance remains. Whenever men are pressured to betray divine truth for the sake of public acceptance, institutional belonging, or economic survival, the Revelation pattern is already visible. The final and fullest expression may yet intensify, but the church must not lose the principle by obsessing over speculative detail. Worship stands at the center. Commerce serves the pressure. The mark signifies allegiance to the beastly worship-order.

Buying and Selling as Economic Coercion

Revelation 13:17 states that no one can buy or sell except the one who has the mark, that is, the name of the beast or the number of its name. This shows that the beastly order does not content itself with inward persuasion or symbolic devotion. It reaches into the ordinary structures of daily life. It seeks to make loyalty economically costly. Buying and selling represent access to social participation, livelihood, provision, and material survival. By tying economic life to allegiance, the beast weaponizes the marketplace. It turns daily necessity into a means of coercion. That is why the mark must be understood not only as identity but also as a mechanism of practical submission.

This does not mean that commerce is the center of the passage, but it does mean commerce is a major instrument of the beastly order. Revelation shows that anti-God power does not operate only through obvious persecution and execution. It also uses exclusion, restriction, and deprivation. A system that can deny people the ability to buy and sell can pressure vast numbers of people into conformity without immediate bloodshed. The beast understands that economic submission can function as moral and religious pressure. Men who would resist open blasphemy may be tempted when food, trade, work, and survival are put at stake. Thus Revelation unveils a harsh truth: false worship is often enforced not only by threats of death but by calculated manipulation of daily necessities.

This pattern makes perfect sense in the broader structure of the chapter. The beast from the sea represents public dominion. The beast from the earth provides deceptive religious justification. The image of the beast institutionalizes idolatry. The mark then individualizes submission to that order, and the buying-and-selling restriction enforces it. In other words, the anti-God system is comprehensive. It seeks political control, religious reverence, institutional form, personal identification, and economic enforcement. Revelation therefore presents not a fragmentary evil but a totalizing order. The beast wants all of life.

The church must see that this economic pressure is not accidental. It is a deliberate strategy of coercion. The beastly order cannot finally create true faithfulness, so it uses material leverage to produce conformity. Men are pushed toward compromise because the cost of resistance is made painfully tangible. The same dynamic has appeared in many lesser forms throughout history whenever loyalty to God has carried occupational loss, public exclusion, confiscation, or economic punishment. Revelation shows that in the final beastly order this principle reaches a sharpened and organized form. Access to trade becomes bound up with visible allegiance.

Yet even here the text still keeps worship at the center. The purpose of restricting buying and selling is not merely to sort the population administratively. It is to enforce participation in the beast's worship-order. Economic pressure serves idolatry. Men are not excluded because the beast cares about efficiency in the abstract. They are excluded because they refuse to belong to the anti-God order. This is why Revelation 20:4 can speak of those who did not worship the beast, did not worship its image, and did not receive the mark. Their refusal included willingness to bear the social and economic cost of fidelity. They preferred suffering with the Lamb over prosperity under the beast.

This is an important pastoral truth for the church. Christians must never assume that faithfulness to Christ will always be economically safe. Revelation teaches the opposite. There may come times when obedience to God means exclusion from the systems by which society ordinarily functions. The mark therefore confronts believers with the issue of ultimate trust. Will one submit to anti-God demands in order to secure earthly provision, or will one remain faithful to God even when buying and selling are cut off? The beast uses economic coercion because material fear is powerful. Revelation calls the holy ones to patient endurance because the pressure will be real. Their security, however, does not lie in the beast's marketplace but in the reign of God and of the Lamb.

The Mark of the Beast Versus the Name of God and the Lamb

The fullest way to understand the mark is to see it in direct contrast to the divine name borne by God's people. Revelation is a book of rival identities, rival allegiances, and rival communities. On one side stand those who belong to God and the Lamb. On the other side stand those who belong to the dragon's order through the beast. The mark of the beast and the name of God and the Lamb are opposing signs of ownership. Revelation 7:3–4 shows God's servants sealed on their foreheads. Revelation 14:1 shows the Lamb's people with His name and His Father's name on their foreheads. By contrast, Revelation 13 shows the beast's followers receiving its mark on forehead or hand. This is one of the strongest interpretive controls in the whole discussion. The mark is not merely an isolated sign of commerce. It is the anti-God counterpart to belonging to God.

This contrast helps explain why the mark is so serious. To receive it is to identify oneself with the beastly order over against the Lamb. To refuse it is to stand with the Lamb even at tremendous cost. Revelation 15:2 shows those who conquered the beast, its image, and the number of its name standing victorious beside the sea of glass. They conquered not by military power but by refusing the beast's claim. They would not take its identity upon themselves. They preferred loyalty to God over ease under the beast. In that sense the mark functions as a dividing line between two humanities, two loyalties, and two destinies.

The divine name and the beastly mark also reveal the deepest issue in Revelation: worshipful belonging. God places His name on His own because they are His redeemed people. The beast places its mark on its own because they belong to the anti-God order. The one leads to preservation, vindication, and life with the Lamb. The other leads to judgment, wrath, and destruction. Revelation 14:9–11 makes this explicit by announcing divine wrath upon those who worship the beast and receive its mark. The contrast is therefore not symbolic ornamentation. It is the contrast between salvation and destruction, fidelity and apostasy, covenant truth and counterfeit allegiance.

This is also why the church must not lose sight of the personal dimension. The beastly order may be vast and institutional, but the mark confronts individuals. Each person must decide where loyalty lies. The world may marvel at the beast, but the faithful bear another name. The world may accept the beast's mark in thought and action, but the holy ones are sealed for God. Revelation therefore drives the question home to the conscience: whose name do you bear, whose claim do you acknowledge, and whose order governs your thinking and your doing? That is the real burden of the text.

Only in that light should the chapter briefly mention the connection to the beast's name and number. Revelation 13:17 says the mark is "the name of the beast or the number of its name." This shows that the mark is tied to identification with the beast itself. The one who bears the mark is marked by the beast's identity. Yet the meaning of the number is not the primary concern here. This chapter must stop where Revelation's own flow suggests it should stop. First the mark is understood as the sign of allegiance to the beastly political-religious order in thought and action, opposed to the name of God and the Lamb. Then the next question naturally arises: what is the meaning of the beast's number, 666? That belongs to the chapter that follows.

For now, the central truth stands in full clarity. The mark of the beast is the sign of allegiance to the anti-God order. It belongs to the realm of worship, identity, and submission before it belongs to the realm of commerce. It reaches the forehead and the hand because it concerns thought and action. It functions as a counter-covenant sign because it opposes the divine name borne by God's people. It is enforced through buying and selling because the beast uses economic coercion to drive conformity. And it stands in direct contrast to the seal and name of God and the Lamb, which mark out the true people of Jehovah. The question Revelation forces upon every reader is not merely whether he can solve a prophetic puzzle. It is whether he will belong to the Lamb or to the beast, whether he will bear God's name or submit to the world's idolatrous claim, and whether he will endure economic and social pressure rather than surrender the worship that belongs to Jehovah alone.

Chapter 13. The Number 666: The Number of a Man and the Meaning of Final Human Rebellion

"Here Is Wisdom"

Revelation 13:18 opens with a summons that immediately governs how the church is to approach the number of the beast: "Here is wisdom. Let the one who has understanding calculate the number of the beast, for it is the number of a man, and his number is 666." That opening line is crucial because it tells us from the start that the number is not given to produce superstition, panic, or speculative excitement. John does not say, "Here is terror," or "Here is mystery without light," but "Here is wisdom." The reader is being called to spiritual discernment shaped by Scripture. Wisdom in Revelation is not curiosity set loose from truth. It is understanding governed by God's revelation. Therefore, the number 666 must be handled with sobriety, biblical perspective, and theological care.

This matters because the number has often been treated in ways that reverse John's intention. Many have approached 666 as though the chief task of the church were to chase hidden codes, identify modern inventions, or match a string of digits to whatever public figure happens to be feared in a given generation. But John's command does not direct the church into endless guessing. It calls the church to understand. The number is meant to reveal something about the beastly order itself. It is not merely a device for excitement. It is part of the unveiling of what the beast really is in the sight of God.

The call for wisdom also reminds the reader that Revelation is a symbolic and theological book. It is saturated with Old Testament imagery, covenantal contrasts, and meaningful numbers. John expects the reader to think in the book's own symbolic world rather than force modern speculation upon the text. The same book that speaks of seven churches, seven lampstands, seven stars, seven seals, seven trumpets, and seven bowls cannot suddenly be treated as though its numbers have no theological weight whenever 666 appears. The number must be read in the same symbolic atmosphere that governs the rest of the Apocalypse.

There is also a pastoral tenderness in the command. The Holy Ones are not being abandoned in confusion. John is not saying that the beast is so dark and so baffling that believers can only tremble before it. He is saying that God has given enough light for the faithful to understand the significance of the beast's number. Wisdom is possible because revelation has been given. The beast may appear terrifying to the world, but heaven has already interpreted it. The number 666 is part of that interpretation. It is not meant to magnify the beast's glory. It is meant to expose the beast's true character.

That opening summons therefore tells the church how to proceed. The right way to read 666 is not with sensation-driven fear, but with scriptural discernment. The right question is not first, "What modern object frightens people?" The right question is, "What does this number reveal about the beastly order in Revelation?" John is not encouraging reckless imagination. He is calling the church to theological understanding. Once that is grasped, much confusion falls away. The number is not a dark charm meant to terrify the saints. It is a divine disclosure meant to unmask final human rebellion.

What It Means to Calculate the Number

John says, "Let the one who has understanding calculate the number of the beast." That language must be interpreted carefully. To calculate does not mean the church is invited into uncontrolled numerological speculation. It does not mean believers should spend their lives attaching the number to endless names, governments, currencies, or inventions as though the prophecy could be exhausted by one successful match. Rather, the command calls for reckoning, considering, and discerning the significance of the number in relation to the beast. The church is to think about what the number means.

This becomes clearer when Revelation 13:16–17 is kept in view. John has already said that the mark is tied to "the name of the beast or the number of its name." The number therefore belongs to the identity of the beastly order. It is not a random numerical tag. It tells the reader something real about the nature of the beast. To calculate the number is to understand why this number belongs to that order and why John presents it as spiritually meaningful. The calculation is therefore theological before it is speculative.

That point is strengthened by the way Revelation uses numbers throughout the book. The seven spirits before the throne in Revelation 1:4, the seven lampstands in Revelation 1:12 and 1:20, the seven seals in Revelation 5:1, the seven horns and seven eyes of the Lamb in Revelation 5:6, the seven angels with seven trumpets in Revelation 8:2, and the seven bowls in Revelation 15:1 all show that numbers in Revelation regularly carry symbolic force. John is not writing a bare statistical report. He is unveiling theological realities in apocalyptic form. It would therefore be unnatural to treat 666 as though it alone must be stripped of symbolic significance and reduced to a code-breaking exercise.

This does not mean that the number has no relation to historical reality. Revelation is not disconnected from history. The beastly order is historical, and its number belongs to its actual identity. But the force of the number is not exhausted by the possibility of connecting it to one passing historical instance. John wrote Revelation to strengthen the Holy Ones across the age of the church, not merely to reward one generation that might finally guess the right contemporary name. The number must therefore carry a meaning broad enough to characterize the beastly order itself and deep enough to remain instructive for the church in every age.

To calculate the number rightly, then, is to reckon the number according to the theological structure of the book. The reader must consider why the beast, this great anti-God order that demands worship, bears the number 666 rather than another number. The answer lies not in panic-driven arithmetic but in spiritual understanding. The number belongs to the beast because it expresses what the beast is: the concentrated expression of fallen humanity in rebellion against Jehovah, aspiring to false fullness, yet forever falling short of divine perfection. That is the calculation that matters. It is the reckoning of the beast's character according to God's own symbolic revelation.

When handled in that way, the command becomes far more useful to the church. Instead of producing endless speculation, it produces theological clarity. The church learns to see the beastly order not as a mystery that must dominate the imagination, but as a rebellion already interpreted by God. The number tells the truth about the beast. It declares that the beast's apparent greatness is counterfeit, its power is creaturely, and its final anti-God order remains stamped with the mark of human deficiency rather than divine fullness.

Why It Is "the Number of a Man"

John explains that the beast's number is "the number of a man." That phrase is one of the most decisive interpretive controls in the verse. Whatever else may be said about 666, the number belongs to man. It is not the number of God. It is not the number of the Lamb. It is not the number of divine fullness. It is the number of a man. This means that the beastly order, however empowered by the dragon, is fundamentally bound up with humanity in rebellion. It is man exalted against God, man organized into anti-God dominion, man seeking worship, man presenting himself as ultimate while remaining creaturely and doomed.

This point is vital because Revelation 13 shows how easily the world is dazzled by the beast. The inhabitants of the earth marvel at it. They worship the dragon because he gave his authority to the beast, and they worship the beast, saying, "Who is like the beast, and who can fight against it?" The world sees invincibility, majesty, and awe. But heaven interprets the matter differently. Heaven says, in effect, the beast's number is the number of a man. That is, the beast remains creaturely. It is not divine. It is not ultimate. It is not what it claims. The number itself strips away the illusion of transcendence and exposes the beast's order as human rebellion in concentrated form.

This phrase also fits perfectly with the larger biblical pattern. In Isaiah 14 the proud one says in his heart that he will ascend and make himself like the Most High, yet he is brought down to Sheol. In Ezekiel 28 the ruler says, "I am a god," yet Jehovah answers that he is a man and not God. In Daniel 11 the self-exalting king magnifies himself above every god. In 2 Thessalonians 2 the man of lawlessness displays himself as being God. The same principle appears again in Revelation. The beastly order strives upward in blasphemous ambition, but God numbers it as man. It is arrogant humanity seeking divine honors, but never escaping human limitation.

The expression "number of a man" also guards the interpreter from two errors. One error is to so individualize the phrase that all its theological force is lost. John is not merely saying, "This belongs to one private human being in a narrow sense." The beast in Revelation is already a larger composite order. Its number therefore belongs to the kind of humanity it embodies. The other error is to so generalize the phrase that all concreteness is lost. Revelation is not speaking of abstraction only. The beastly order is historical, visible, and embodied in real structures of power. Thus the phrase best points to humanity in organized rebellion, humanity gathered into a mature anti-God order, humanity claiming greatness beyond creaturely limits while still bearing the stamp of man rather than God.

That is why this phrase is so devastating to the beast's pretensions. The beast seeks worship. It claims public reverence. It mimics false fullness. Yet its number exposes it as man-centered rebellion. The anti-God order may appear irresistible, but it is the number of a man. It may gather kings and nations, but it is the number of a man. It may demand worship and persecute the faithful, but it is still the number of a man. John is therefore not increasing the beast's mystery so much as reducing its false majesty. The number humiliates the beast by revealing its true nature.

This is also why the church should take courage from the phrase. The beast is powerful, but not divine. The beast is terrifying, but not transcendent. The beast is dragonically energized, yet still numbered as man. By contrast, the Lamb is the One who shares the throne, the slain and risen Lord, the faithful Witness, the Firstborn from the dead, the Ruler of the kings of the earth. The number of the beast points downward to rebellious humanity. The glory of the Lamb points upward to true sovereignty. The contrast is total, and the church must see it clearly.

Six, Seven, and Symbolic Deficiency

The theological force of 666 becomes clearer when it is read against the repeated use of seven in Revelation. The number seven is one of the great structuring symbols of the book. Revelation opens with seven churches, seven spirits, seven lampstands, and seven stars. It proceeds through seven seals, seven trumpets, and seven bowls. The Lamb is described with seven horns and seven eyes. The whole book is ordered by seven-patterns that communicate fullness, completeness, and divinely ordered totality. In Revelation's symbolic world, seven is consistently associated with what is complete in the purpose of God.

Against that background, six carries a fitting significance. Six falls short of seven. It comes near, but does not attain fullness. It approaches completeness, yet remains deficient. In ordinary arithmetic, of course, six is simply a number. But in the symbolic structure of Revelation, set against the recurring seven-patterns of the book, six becomes a fitting number for what lacks divine completeness. It signifies falling short, imperfection, and deficiency relative to the fullness symbolized by seven.

Once that is seen, 666 takes on its proper theological force. The beast is not merely marked by six once, but by six threefold. The deficiency is intensified. The falling short is brought to climactic expression. The beastly order presents itself as though it were complete, total, and worthy of universal allegiance. But its number reveals the opposite. It is the concentrated expression of what never reaches divine fullness. It is man in rebellion multiplied in its arrogance, deepened in its corruption, and organized in its anti-God ambition, yet still only six, not seven. However complete the beast may appear in the eyes of the world, heaven marks it as radically and utterly falling short.

This reading also fits the beast's role in the chapter. The beast is a counterfeit kingdom. It imitates authority, receives worship, and presents a false claim to finality. It seeks to rival what belongs to God and the Lamb. But counterfeit glory is not real glory. False fullness is not true fullness. The number 666 therefore functions as heaven's judgment on the beast's pretension. It says, in effect, this order aspires to total dominion, but it remains the intensified number of human failure. It mimics fullness, but it is the fullness of rebellion, not the fullness of God.

The threefold form of the number deepens that emphasis. Revelation often uses repetition for intensity. "Holy, holy, holy" expresses supreme holiness. "Woe, woe, woe" signals intensified judgment. In the same symbolic atmosphere, 666 points to intensified deficiency. It is not casual repetition. It is emphatic. The beastly order is not mildly imperfect. It is mature rebellion. It is man in climactic anti-God form. It is human incompleteness hardened into organized defiance of Jehovah. That is why the number suits the beast so well. It exposes the order as the mature expression of fallen man seeking divine place while remaining under creaturely judgment.

This symbolic deficiency also helps explain why the number is joined to the mark and the name of the beast. The mark signifies allegiance to the beastly order. The number interprets the order to which the marked belong. They bear the sign of a system that is fundamentally incomplete, corrupt, and anti-God. The number therefore does not merely identify the beast; it interprets the whole reality of beastly dominion. It tells the church what the anti-God order really is in the sight of heaven: a climactic but deficient counterfeit of true fullness.

The seven-patterns of Revelation make this especially compelling. The seven spirits before God's throne, the seven lampstands among which Christ walks, the seven seals in the hand of the One on the throne, the seven horns and seven eyes of the Lamb, the seven trumpets, and the seven bowls all belong to the ordered fullness of God's redemptive and judicial purpose. Set against that repeated use of seven, the beast's 666 stands out as a dark parody. It reaches for totality, yet it is not totality in God's sense. It reaches for perfection, yet it is forever falling short. It is completeness only in the sense of complete rebellion.

Why 666 Should Not Be Reduced to Numerological Panic

Because the number is striking and memorable, it has often been mishandled in ways that produce fear rather than wisdom. This must be rejected. John did not give the number so that the church would become consumed with numerical panic. He gave it so that the church would understand the beast. Yet many interpreters have done the opposite. They have encouraged believers to fear digits, to suspect every appearance of the number, and to chase endless identifications as though the chief duty of Christian watchfulness were constant numerological alarm. That approach not only creates confusion; it also empties the number of its real theological force.

The great problem with numerological panic is that it detaches 666 from the context John himself gives it. Revelation 13 is about the beast, false worship, the mark, and allegiance to an anti-God order. The number belongs to that setting. It is part of the theological exposure of the beastly system. When Christians treat the number as though it were a free-floating source of dread, they may end up fearing arithmetic more than false worship. They may become preoccupied with codes while missing John's real warning about beastly allegiance, deception, and rebellion. That is not wisdom. It is distraction.

Revelation 14:9–11 helps keep the matter straight. Judgment falls on those who worship the beast and its image and receive its mark. Revelation 15:2 praises those who conquered the beast, its image, and the number of its name. Revelation 20:4 honors those who did not worship the beast or its image and did not receive its mark. In all these passages, the focus is not on irrational fear of numbers but on fidelity in the face of false worship and coercive allegiance. The number belongs to that larger issue. It is serious because it is tied to the beast's identity and order, not because it is a magical object of terror.

Numerological panic also tends to magnify the beast in the imagination of believers. It can make evil seem mysterious, limitless, and almost omnipresent. But Revelation does not give the number to exalt the beast. It gives the number to expose the beast. The number 666 is not a badge of invincibility. It is a mark of deficiency. It is heaven's way of saying that the beast's order, however impressive it looks, remains bound to the limits of rebellious humanity. The church therefore dishonors the text when it treats 666 as though it were a source of superstition rather than a revelation of the beast's falling-short condition.

There is another pastoral danger here. Sensational treatments of 666 can train believers to look for the wrong thing. Instead of watching for organized rebellion against God, false worship, anti-Christian allegiance, and counterfeit fullness, they may watch only for isolated outward patterns that can be numerically dramatized. That approach reduces discernment to fear-driven guesswork. But John calls for understanding, not frenzy. The church must ask whether a system exalts man against God, whether it demands allegiance contrary to the Lamb, whether it marks people for participation in anti-God order, and whether it embodies counterfeit fullness in rebellion. Those are the real concerns of the text.

This does not mean the number is unimportant. It is profoundly important. But its importance lies in what it means, not in the panic it can generate. The number 666 reveals the beastly order as mature human rebellion, intensified deficiency, and organized anti-God pretension. The church must understand that and refuse allegiance to it. That is a far more serious matter than endless speculation over hidden codes. John wants faithful endurance, not numerological obsession. He wants the Holy Ones to see through the beast's apparent greatness and remain with the Lamb.

The right response, therefore, is neither dismissiveness nor panic. It is sober understanding. The church should neither ignore the number nor idolize it. It should receive it as part of God's unveiling of final human rebellion. The beast is numbered, interpreted, and judged by heaven. Its power is real, but its nature is exposed. Its claims are loud, but its deficiency is fixed. Its order is impressive to the world, but God has already declared it to be 666, the concentrated number of man in rebellion rather than the fullness of God.

The Number as the Interpretation of the Whole Order

The number 666 does not stand in Revelation as a detached curiosity or as a puzzle meant chiefly to provoke speculative code-breaking. It interprets the beastly order itself. It shows that the final political-religious system opposed to Jehovah is the mature embodiment of fallen humanity in rebellion. It is called a man's number because it belongs to man in arrogant independence from God, not to divine perfection. Since seven signifies fullness or completeness in Revelation's symbolic world, six signifies falling short; and when intensified in a threefold form, 666 denotes intensified human incompleteness, corruption, and anti-God self-exaltation. The number therefore exposes the beast's apparent greatness as counterfeit. However powerful and impressive that order may seem, it is not divine fullness. It is man in rebellion organized into a climactic anti-God structure and therefore doomed by the very imperfection it cannot overcome.

This is why the number belongs so naturally with the mark. The mark identifies those who belong to the beastly order in thought and action. The number interprets the order to which they belong.

Together they show that the anti-God system seeks covenant-like loyalty, public identity, and practical submission, yet all of it belongs to a kingdom of falling-short rebellion rather than the fullness of God. The marked belong to an order that appears mighty but bears the number of deficiency. They serve a kingdom that presents itself as final but remains creaturely, corrupt, and condemned.

Revelation 17:8–14 underscores this same truth. The beast astonishes the dwellers on the earth. Kings unite with it. The nations are drawn into its rebellion. Yet the Lamb overcomes them because He is Lord of lords and King of kings. The number 666 belongs in that same contrast. The beast is the gathered fullness of rebellious humanity, but the Lamb is true sovereignty. The beast's order is climactic in wickedness, but not ultimate in power. The number itself says so. It bears the stamp of man, not God; of six, not seven; of counterfeit fullness, not true completion.

Revelation 14:9–11 adds the final moral gravity. Those who worship the beast and receive its mark come under the wrath of God. That judgment fits the number's meaning. 666 is not merely descriptive of human rebellion; it belongs to a rebellion already marked out for divine wrath. What falls short of God while exalting itself against Him does not move toward lasting glory. It moves toward judgment. The number is therefore also a warning. It tells the church what kind of kingdom the beast offers and what end that kingdom brings.

Thus the number 666 must be handled theologically, not sensationally. It is the number of a man because the beastly order is humanity in final organized rebellion. It is six threefold because it signifies intensified deficiency and perfected falling short. It stands over against Revelation's many sevens because the beast is a false fullness, a parody of totality, a kingdom of pretension rather than divine completeness. And it belongs with the mark because the marked identify themselves with that whole anti-God order.

The church should therefore read 666 with wisdom and courage. The beast may appear vast, but its number reveals its limits. The beast may demand worship, but its number exposes its humanity. The beast may gather kings and nations, but its number shows that its seeming fullness is only the fullness of rebellion. The Lamb alone possesses true glory, true dominion, and true completeness. The Holy Ones must therefore refuse the beast's claim, reject the counterfeit, endure in loyalty to Christ, and remember that heaven has already interpreted the number of the final anti-God order. It is 666: the number of a man, the number of intensified falling short, and the number of humanity in climactic rebellion against Jehovah, soon to be crushed by the victorious reign of the Lamb.

Edward D. Andrews

Part Five: The Victory of Christ Over the Entire Antichristic Order

Chapter 14. The Destruction of the Lawless and Beastly Order at Christ's Coming

Christ Slays the Lawless One

The closing movement of this book must begin where Paul himself places the emphasis: not on the temporary success of the lawless one, but on the certainty of his destruction by the returning Christ. Second Thessalonians 2:8 states with unmistakable clarity, "then the lawless one will be revealed, whom the Lord Jesus will slay with the breath of His mouth and bring to nothing by the appearance of His coming." That sentence is one of the great deathblows to every form of fear-driven interpretation. However dark the apostasy becomes, however arrogant the lawless one appears, and however persuasive his deception may be among those who do not love the truth, his entire career is bounded by the appearing of Jesus Christ. The lawless one is not an equal rival to the Son of God. He is a doomed rebel waiting for the public manifestation of the King.

Paul's wording deserves careful attention. He says the Lord Jesus will slay him "with the breath of His mouth." This language reaches back to Isaiah 11:4, where the Messianic ruler "will strike the earth with the rod of his mouth, and with the breath of his lips he will kill the wicked." The point is not that Christ's victory is somehow weak or merely symbolic. The point is that His judicial word is sovereign, irresistible, and final. The same Christ who created by divine authority, who taught with heavenly authority, and who now reigns in exalted authority will overthrow the whole lawless pretension by His own royal power. The usurper who exalts himself in the sphere of worship is undone not by gradual human reform, not by political negotiation, and not by the self-collapse of history alone, but by the active intervention of the glorified Christ.

This is why the lawless one must never be studied apart from the Second Coming. Paul does not describe the man of lawlessness in order to enthrone him in the imagination of believers. He describes him in order to reveal the seriousness of apostasy and then to show the certainty of Christ's triumph over that apostasy in its concentrated form. The lawless one is terrifying only when looked at in isolation. When viewed in the light of Christ's appearing, he is exposed as temporary, creaturely, and already sentenced. He may display himself as being God, but the true Lord appears and reduces him to nothing. He may sit in the sphere of worship, but he cannot survive the appearing of the One to whom all worship truly belongs.

The phrase "bring to nothing by the appearance of His coming" deepens the certainty. Christ does not merely wound the lawless order; He nullifies it. He renders it powerless, strips it of all pretended majesty, and ends its blasphemous claim. What the world had feared, admired, or submitted to is exposed as empty before the unveiled glory of the Son. This is one of the great themes of biblical eschatology: evil often appears strongest just before it is overthrown. The lawless one reaches revealed form, but only in order to be publicly destroyed. His exposure is itself part of the divine road to judgment. Jehovah allows the rebellion to ripen so that its defeat may be decisive and its condemnation unmistakably just.

This also gathers together the line already traced from Daniel. Daniel 11 presented the self-exalting king who magnifies himself above every god. Second Thessalonians 2 presents the man of lawlessness who exalts himself in the temple of God. But Paul does not leave the reader staring at the usurper. He pushes the eye beyond him to the appearing of Christ. Daniel had already said that the arrogant ruler prospers only until the indignation is complete, because what is decreed must be done. Paul now reveals the climactic moment of that decree: the Lord Jesus Himself appears, and the lawless boast is silenced forever. All antichristic usurpation collapses at the presence of the Messiah.

The church must therefore hear this opening truth with full force. The lawless one is real, apostasy is real, deception is real, and the rebellion reaches terrible maturity. Yet Christ's appearing is more real, more powerful, and final. The last horizon of prophecy is not a triumphant antichristic order, but the unveiled Messiah destroying every false claimant to religious supremacy. The church does not await the endless reign of lawlessness. It awaits the appearing of the Lord Jesus Christ, who by the breath of His mouth slays the lawless one and brings his whole arrogant project to nothing.

The Beast and the Kings of the Earth Defeated

What Paul says in concentrated form concerning the lawless one, Revelation unfolds in majestic detail concerning the beast and the kings of the earth. Revelation 17:14 states, "These will wage war against the Lamb, and the Lamb will conquer them, because He is Lord of lords and King of kings, and those with Him are called and chosen and faithful." That verse gathers into one line the central conflict of history. The kings of the earth, acting in harmony with the beastly order, do not merely oppose biblical morality or the church as a social presence. They wage war against the Lamb. Their rebellion is fundamentally Christological. It is opposition to the Messiah Himself, to His rule, and to the people who belong to Him. Yet the outcome is declared before the battle is described in full: the Lamb conquers them.

This conquering Christ is then shown openly in Revelation 19:11–21. John sees heaven opened, and behold, a white horse, with the rider called Faithful and True. In righteousness He judges and wages war. His eyes are a flame of fire. He wears many diadems. He is clothed in a robe dipped in blood, and His name is called the Word of God. The armies of heaven follow Him. From His mouth comes a sharp sword with which to strike down the nations, and He will shepherd them with a rod of iron. The imagery is rich, but the theological center is plain: the returning Christ is the warrior King whose judgment is righteous, whose authority is absolute, and whose victory is certain.

This passage must be read in direct relation to Psalm 2:9, where Jehovah says of His Anointed, "You shall break them with a rod of iron and dash them in pieces like a potter's vessel." Revelation 19 shows the fulfillment of that royal decree. The nations had raged against Jehovah and His Anointed. The kings of the earth had set themselves against the Lamb. The beast had gathered armies. Yet the Messiah comes not as a suffering servant now, but as the reigning King executing holy judgment. The rod of iron is no empty metaphor. It signifies the irresistible rule of the Son over every rebellious power. No beastly empire, no alliance of kings, and no organized antichristic system can withstand Him.

The defeat itself is described with deliberate severity. The beast is captured, and with it the false prophet who had performed signs in its presence, by which he deceived those who had received the mark of the beast and worshiped its image. These two are thrown alive into the lake of fire that burns with sulfur. The rest are slain by the sword coming from the mouth of the rider on the horse. This shows that the beastly order, the deceptive religious order, and the rebellious rulers of the earth all fall together under Christ's judgment. No branch of the anti-God system survives. Political rebellion, false worship, deceitful signs, and idolatrous allegiance are all brought to one end before the appearing of the King.

This matters greatly for the theology of the whole book. We have distinguished the antichristic principle, the apostasy, the man of lawlessness, the beast from the sea, the beast from the earth, the image of the beast, the mark, and the number. Those distinctions matter and must be preserved. Yet here at the end all these rebellious streams are gathered into one final overthrow. The anti-God order in all its dimensions is judged together. The lawless religious usurpation Paul exposed, the beastly political-religious order John exposed, and the arrogant dominion Daniel exposed all meet the same end: destruction at the coming of Christ.

This also provides the necessary emotional and theological balance for the church. Revelation does not reveal the beast so that believers will live in dread of beastly power. It reveals the beast so that they will see it judged by the returning Christ. The kings of the earth are real, their rage is real, their gathered war is real, but the Lamb's conquest is greater than all of it. He is not merely another combatant in the field. He is Lord of lords and King of kings. His victory is not uncertain. It is the inevitable outworking of His sovereign identity. The beast may gather the nations, but the Lamb conquers them because He is the rightful ruler of all rulers. The last word over empire belongs to Christ.

The Final Doom of Satanic Deception

Revelation does not stop with the destruction of the beast and the false prophet. It pushes the reader to the final doom of the dragon himself. Revelation 20:10 says, "the devil who deceived them was thrown into the lake of fire and sulfur where the beast and the false prophet were also; and they will be tormented day and night forever and ever." This verse is the end of the entire satanic project. It answers every earlier chapter in one final act of divine judgment. The dragon's war in Revelation 12, the beastly order of Revelation 13, the gathering of kings in Revelation 17, and the war of Revelation 19 all terminate here. The deceiver himself is judged.

That fact is essential because it shows that biblical prophecy is not content merely to remove secondary agents while leaving the primary source untouched. The false prophet falls. The beast falls. The kings fall. But the dragon must also fall, because the anti-God order in history is animated by satanic deception. Revelation 20:10 therefore stands as the complete answer to the lie. The serpent who deceived in Eden, the dragon who persecuted the woman and her offspring, and the one who gave the beast his power, throne, and great authority is finally cast into irreversible judgment. There is no recovery from this sentence. There is no renewed rebellion after this doom. The deceiver's end is fixed forever.

This is where the whole theme of deception comes to rest. Earlier chapters showed the spirit of antichrist, false prophets, lying signs, the deception of those who do not love the truth, and the false wonders used to lead men into beast-worship. Revelation now says that the deceiver himself is condemned. Every counterfeit sign, every false claim, every lying wonder, every deceptive religious structure, and every beastly parody of divine authority stands behind the dragon's work and therefore shares in the dragon's sentence. The judgment is not partial. It reaches the source.

The church must see this clearly because satanic deception often appears durable in history. Error can seem to spread. False religion can seem powerful. Beastly systems can seem immovable. But Revelation 20:10 tells the church what all of it is moving toward. Satan's strategy does not culminate in final victory. It culminates in final punishment. His deception is not a rival kingdom that will endure beside God's kingdom. It is a condemned rebellion whose entire structure is temporary and already appointed for the lake of fire.

There is also a profound comfort here for the faithful. The Holy Ones have often suffered not merely from human rulers but from the deeper malice of the devil who works through those rulers and false teachers. Persecution, seduction, slander, false worship, and economic pressure all bear the marks of a deeper spiritual enemy. Revelation therefore gives the saints more than the destruction of visible persecutors. It gives them the destruction of the invisible adversary behind them. The dragon who made war against the offspring of the woman is himself judged. The church does not merely outlast Satan; it lives to see his project utterly undone by the righteousness of God.

This final doom also clarifies why every antichristic power is temporary. The dragon is the source of the anti-God order, yet even he is not beyond judgment. If Satan himself cannot escape Christ's reign, then none of his instruments can possibly endure. Every beast, every false prophet, every lawless pretender, and every deceptive structure is already under a sentence that reaches back to the throne of

God and forward to the final day. The doom of satanic deception is therefore the deepest guarantee that the last word cannot belong to antichristic power. The whole rebellious order is already mortally judged because its source is judged.

The Kingdom Given to the Holy Ones

Daniel 7 provides one of the clearest Old Testament summaries of the entire prophetic trajectory. After the beastly powers rage, after the little horn speaks great things and wears down the holy ones, after judgment sits and dominion is taken away, Daniel says, "the kingdom and the dominion and the greatness of the kingdoms under the whole heaven shall be given to the people of the holy ones of the Most High; His kingdom shall be an everlasting kingdom, and all dominions shall serve and obey Him" (Daniel 7:26–27). This is one of the most important truths for bringing the whole book to its proper close. Christ's victory is not merely negative, as though He destroys the beastly order and leaves a void. His victory is positive. The kingdom is given to the holy ones under His everlasting reign.

This passage unites perfectly with 1 Corinthians 15:24–28. Paul says that the end comes when Christ hands over the kingdom to God the Father after abolishing all rule and all authority and power. He must reign until He has put all His enemies under His feet. The last enemy to be abolished is death. Then all things are subjected under Him so that God may be all in all. That Pauline language belongs naturally beside Daniel 7. Beastly dominion is abolished. Rebellious authority is brought down. Enemy power is crushed. And then the kingdom in its consummate order stands openly under God through the victorious reign of Christ. The church must not miss this. Biblical prophecy does not move from beast to emptiness. It moves from beastly usurpation to Messianic order.

The giving of the kingdom to the holy ones also reveals the vindication of the faithful. Throughout the prophetic narrative, the holy ones have been oppressed, deceived, marginalized, excluded, and often killed. Daniel's little horn made war with them. The beast of Revelation made war on them. The dragon raged against them. The economic coercion of the mark sought to break them. Yet the end is not the everlasting humiliation of the saints. The end is the inheritance of the kingdom. Those who suffered under beastly rule will reign under Christ's righteous dominion. Those whom the world considered weak are publicly vindicated as the true heirs of the kingdom.

This also helps guard the church from a merely defensive eschatology. The faithful are not called only to endure until evil collapses. They are called to endure in hope of an everlasting kingdom. Their future is not bare survival. It is participation in Christ's triumph. That is why Revelation 17:14 says those with the Lamb are "called and chosen and faithful." Their faithfulness is not wasted. It is the path of those who belong to the victorious King. Daniel 7:27 then shows the public answer to all their suffering: the kingdom is given to the holy ones of the Most High.

The everlasting nature of this kingdom must also be emphasized. Beastly dominion is temporary. The little horn has a set span. The lawless one is destroyed by the appearing of Christ. The beast and false prophet are cast into the lake of fire. Satan himself is judged. But the kingdom of Christ and His holy ones is everlasting. It does not rise and fall in succession like the kingdoms of men. It does not depend on dragonic power. It does not imitate life while carrying death within itself. It is the true kingdom under the reign of the Son, established in righteousness and secured forever by the purpose of Jehovah.

That is why Daniel 7 remains so necessary at the end of this book. It shows that the beastly order, for all its terror, is never the final form of history. The final form of history is the reign of God through His Christ, shared with the holy ones whom He has redeemed and preserved. The church must therefore read all prophecies of antichristic opposition in the light of this inheritance. The Holy Ones are not destined for permanent defeat. They are destined for the kingdom. That truth alone gives prophetic endurance its right shape. The saints resist the beast because the kingdom belongs to them in Christ.

Why the Last Word Belongs to Christ, Not Antichrist

The final chapter of this book must make one thing unmistakably plain: the last word belongs to Christ, not antichrist. Every earlier chapter has exposed some aspect of the anti-God order. We have seen many antichrists already at work. We have seen apostasy within the professing sphere. We have seen the man of lawlessness, the beastly political-religious order, the mark of the beast, and the number 666. All of those matters are necessary. Scripture reveals them because believers must understand the shape of rebellion. But none of them is the final center of biblical prophecy. The center is the victorious Messiah. Evil is revealed so that Christ may be seen conquering it.

Psalm 2 already established this from the beginning. The nations rage. The peoples meditate on emptiness. The kings of the earth take their stand against Jehovah and His Anointed. Yet Jehovah says, "I have installed My King upon Zion, My holy mountain." The Son is given the nations as His inheritance. He breaks rebellion with a rod of iron. The psalm does not end with the kings' conspiracy. It ends with the Son's supremacy and a call to submit to Him. That same movement controls the whole prophetic witness of Scripture. The Bible reveals the rage of the nations, the arrogance of rulers, the deceit of false religion, and the fury of satanic rebellion, but only so that the triumph of the Son may stand out more clearly.

Second Thessalonians 2 ends the same way. Revelation 17 ends the same way. Revelation 19 ends the same way. Revelation 20 ends the same way. Daniel 7 ends the same way. In every case, the anti-God order is temporary, judged, and doomed. The Son of God remains. The Lamb remains. The kingdom remains. The Holy Ones remain. The antichristic powers do not write the conclusion of the story. Christ does.

This is essential not only theologically but pastorally. If a reader dwells on antichristic power without reaching Christ's victory, he may become fearful, fascinated, or spiritually off-center. Scripture does not deny the terror of the enemy, but it constantly reorients the believer toward the Lord's triumph. The church must therefore refuse every interpretation of prophecy that leaves the emotional and theological center on the beast, the lawless one, or the dragon. The true center is the Messiah who slays the lawless one, defeats the beast, casts down the false prophet, destroys the dragon, and gives the kingdom to the holy ones.

This also gives proper perspective to every present conflict. Antichristic power is real, but it is not ultimate. Apostasy is real, but it is not final. Beastly coercion is real, but it is not everlasting. Economic exclusion is real, but it cannot cut believers off from the inheritance of the kingdom. Deception is real, but it cannot overturn the truth established in Christ. Even death itself is not ultimate, because Christ abolishes the last enemy and reigns until all things are subjected under Him. Once that is understood, the church can endure without despair. The faithful do not endure because they are naturally strong. They endure because they know who wins.

The final word belongs to Christ because He alone is the true King. He alone is Faithful and True. He alone is the Lamb who was slain and now reigns. He alone is Lord of lords and King of kings. He alone destroys every anti-God power by His appearing. He alone receives the everlasting kingdom. And He alone shares that kingdom with His holy ones. No beast can rival that. No lawless one can withstand that. No dragon can escape that. The entire antichristic order, in all its forms, rises under divine limit, matures under divine observation, and falls under divine judgment before the victorious Messiah.

Therefore this book must end where Scripture ends the matter: with the triumph of Jesus Christ. The anti-God order is real, but it is temporary. The rebellion is intense, but it is doomed. The deception is widespread, but it is judged. The beast may rage, the kings may gather, the lawless one may exalt himself, and the dragon may deceive, but the Lamb conquers. Christ slays the lawless one. Christ defeats the beast and the kings of the earth. Christ consigns the false prophet and the devil to final judgment. Christ receives and manifests the everlasting kingdom. Christ gives that kingdom to the holy ones. And because that is true, the church can read every prophecy of antichristic opposition with sober realism, holy courage, and unwavering confidence. The last word does not belong to antichrist. The last word belongs to Jesus Christ.

Glossary of Terms

A

Abomination of Desolation

A desecrating intrusion into the sphere of worship, first set forth in Daniel and then taken up by Jesus in His prophetic discourse. It refers to an anti-God profanation that invades what belongs to Jehovah and marks the advance of rebellious power into the holy sphere.

Abyss

The place of restraint and confinement associated in Revelation with demonic and satanic imprisonment. It is not the final lake of fire, but a place of divinely imposed limitation prior to final judgment.

Adversary

A biblical description of Satan as the one who opposes God, resists His people, and seeks to destroy their faithfulness through deception, accusation, persecution, and false worship.

Allegiance

The inward and outward loyalty a person gives to a ruler, kingdom, or order. In Revelation, allegiance is never merely political. It is spiritual, moral, and worshipful, involving thought, confession, obedience, and public identification.

Apostasy

A deliberate falling away from revealed truth within the professing sphere of faith. Apostasy is not mere weakness or confusion. It is defection from apostolic teaching, especially concerning Jesus Christ and the gospel.

Appearance of His Coming

Paul's phrase in 2 Thessalonians 2:8 for the public manifestation of Christ in glory, by which He destroys the lawless one and brings the anti-God order to nothing.

Armageddon

The symbolic gathering place of the kings of the earth under satanic deception for final conflict against God and His Christ. It represents the climactic concentration of rebellious worldly power before divine judgment.

Authority

The rightful power to rule, command, and judge. Scripture presents all true authority as deriving from God, while the beastly order is marked by illegitimate, self-exalting, and dragonically energized authority.

B

Babylon the Great

The symbolic name in Revelation for the great world-order of false religion, spiritual corruption, and anti-God seduction allied with beastly power. She represents organized unfaithfulness, idolatry, and hostility to God's truth.

Beast

In prophetic symbolism, a beast represents anti-God dominion in its violent, arrogant, and rebellious form. In Revelation, the beast is the mature political-religious order energized by the dragon and set against God, His Christ, and His people.

Beast From the Earth

The second beast in Revelation 13, later identified as the false prophet. It is the deceptive religious agent that promotes worship of the first beast, performs signs, and enforces loyalty to the beastly order.

Beast From the Sea

The first beast in Revelation 13, the mature political expression of dragonic power. It is the final concentration of Daniel's beastly empire pattern, demanding submission, blaspheming God, and making war on the holy ones.

Blasphemy

Speech or action that dishonors Jehovah, usurps what belongs to Him, or exalts the creature against the Creator. In prophecy, blasphemy is a central mark of the beastly and lawless order.

Book of Life

The divine register of those who belong to the Lamb and inherit salvation. In Revelation, those whose names are written in the book of life stand in contrast to the world that marvels after the beast.

Breath of His Mouth

A figure for Christ's sovereign judicial word by which He destroys the lawless one. It points to the irresistible authority of the Messiah to judge and overthrow every rebel power.

C

Calling

God's effectual summons by which He brings His people into relationship with Himself through Christ. In Revelation 17:14, those with the Lamb are described as called, chosen, and faithful.

Christ

The Messiah, the Anointed One promised in the Scriptures and fulfilled in Jesus. All antichristic and beastly opposition is ultimately opposition to Jehovah's Christ and His rightful kingship.

Christological Error

False teaching concerning the person, identity, nature, or work of Jesus Christ. In John's writings, such error is central to the doctrine of antichrist because denial of the Son is rebellion against both the Son and the Father.

Church

The congregation of believers who belong to Christ, hold to the apostolic faith, and bear witness to Him in the world. In this book's framework, the visible sphere of the church must be distinguished from mere outward profession.

Commerce

The economic exchange of buying and selling. In Revelation 13, commerce becomes an instrument of coercion by which the beastly order pressures people into outward conformity and anti-God allegiance.

Counter-Covenant Identity

A false identity imposed by the anti-God order in imitation of God's covenant claim over His people. The mark of the beast is counter-covenant because it stands opposite the divine name borne by God's servants.

Counterfeit Wonder

A deceptive sign or display that mimics divine power while serving falsehood, false worship, and rebellion. Scripture warns that false prophets and the beastly order use such wonders to mislead many.

Covenant Loyalty

Faithful devotion to Jehovah and His revealed will. In the prophetic context of this book, covenant loyalty is tested under pressure from apostasy, persecution, false worship, and beastly coercion.

D

Danielic Pattern

The prophetic structure found in Daniel involving beastly empire, arrogant rulers, persecution of the holy ones, desecration, and divine judgment. This pattern stands behind later teaching in Paul and Revelation.

Day of the Lord

The time of divine intervention, judgment, and vindication associated with Christ's coming. In 2 Thessalonians, Paul corrects false claims about that day by explaining that the apostasy and the revealing of the lawless one must come first.

Deceiver

One who leads others away from the truth of God, especially concerning Jesus Christ. In John's letters, the deceiver is closely tied to antichrist because false teaching about Christ is central to the antichristic lie.

Deception

The satanic distortion of truth in order to mislead people into false belief, false worship, and rebellion against God. In the final anti-God order, deception works through doctrine, signs, wonders, and institutional pressure.

Desecration

The profaning of what belongs to Jehovah. In prophecy, desecration often refers to anti-God intrusion into the sphere of worship, where rebellious power seeks to defile the holy order of God.

Dragon

The symbolic name in Revelation for Satan, the ancient serpent, the devil. He is the unseen source behind the beastly order and wages war against God's people through deception, persecution, and counterfeit authority.

Divine Name

The name of Jehovah placed upon His people as a sign of belonging, ownership, and covenant identity. In Revelation, the divine name stands in deliberate contrast to the mark and name of the beast.

Dominion

Rule, power, and governing authority. Scripture contrasts beastly dominion, which is arrogant and rebellious, with the righteous everlasting dominion of Christ.

E

Economic Coercion

The use of buying, selling, work, and material survival as instruments of pressure to force conformity to an anti-God order. In Revelation 13, this is one of the chief functions of the mark of the beast.

Election

A biblical term often used for God's choosing of His people. The emphasis in this work is better expressed by terms such as chosen, called, or belonging to God rather than by later doctrinal systems.

Empire

A large public order of human dominion. In Daniel and Revelation, empire becomes beastly when it exalts itself against God, persecutes the holy ones, and seeks to replace divine authority with creaturely power.

Endurance

The steadfast faithfulness of God's people under pressure, persecution, deception, and exclusion. Revelation repeatedly calls the holy ones to endurance because beastly power is real but temporary.

Eschatology

The study of last things or final things in God's purpose. In this book, eschatology is centered on Christ's triumph over apostasy, lawlessness, beastly dominion, and satanic deception.

Eternal Destruction

The final and irreversible judgment of the wicked. In the framework of this book, it does not mean everlasting conscious life in torment as a natural possession, but final ruin under the judgment of God.

F

Faithful Witness

A title associated with Christ and, by extension, with those who testify truly about Him. Faithful witness stands over against false prophecy, lying wonders, and beastly propaganda.

False Christ

Any claimant who presents himself in the place of Christ or against Christ. Jesus warned that many false christs would arise, and John's doctrine of antichrist is closely related to that warning.

False Prophet

The deceptive religious voice that supports anti-God power and leads people into false worship. In Revelation, the false prophet corresponds to the beast from the earth and is closely connected with signs and the image of the beast.

False Worship

Reverence, devotion, and submission directed toward what is not God. In Revelation, false worship reaches its climax in the worship of the dragon, the beast, and the image of the beast.

Falling Away

Another expression for apostasy. It emphasizes departure from revealed truth after outward contact with that truth has already occurred.

Forehead

A biblical symbol of visible identity, conscious loyalty, and covenantal marking. In Revelation, the forehead is where the divine name or the beastly mark identifies a person as belonging to one side or the other.

Foundation of the Apostles and Prophets

he once-for-all doctrinal foundation laid in the church through Christ's appointed messengers. In this book's argument, apostolic presence and authority function as a restraining force against the full manifestation of lawlessness.

G

Gathering of the Kings

The uniting of earthly rulers under beastly and dragonic influence in opposition to the Lamb. Revelation shows this as the final concentration of worldly rebellion before Christ's overthrow of the anti-God order.

Gehenna

The place or image of final destruction in biblical usage. Gehenna signifies irreversible ruin rather than the preservation of eternal conscious life in judgment.

Glorified Christ

Jesus Christ after His resurrection, ascension, and exaltation, now reigning in heavenly glory and destined to return in open triumph over all anti-God power.

Gog and Magog

Symbols in Revelation 20 for the final gathering of rebellious nations under satanic deception against the people of God before divine judgment falls.

Great Tribulation

A time of severe distress, persecution, and testing associated with the conflict between the kingdom of God and the anti-God order. In prophetic interpretation, it must be read with care and in context.

H

Hand

A biblical symbol of action, obedience, labor, and practical service. In Revelation, the mark on the hand signifies outward participation in and practical conformity to the beastly order.

Heavenly Worship

The pure worship rendered in the heavenly court to Jehovah and to the Lamb. Revelation constantly contrasts heavenly worship with beast-worship on earth.

Holy Ones

The people of God set apart to Him through Christ. This term is preferable to "saints" in this book's framework and is especially important in Daniel and Revelation, where the holy ones suffer under beastly oppression but inherit the kingdom.

Horn

A prophetic symbol of power, kingly authority, or ruling strength. In Daniel and Revelation, horns often signify kingdoms, rulers, or concentrated authority within a broader anti-God system.

I

Idolatry

The worship of anything other than Jehovah. In the prophetic setting of this book, idolatry reaches final organized expression in the worship of the beast and its image.

Image of the Beast

The institutionalized form of beast-worship. It is the visible and enforced embodiment of the anti-God order, used to demand public idolatrous allegiance and punish refusal.

Incarnation

The coming of Jesus Christ in the flesh. John identifies denial of the incarnation as one of the clearest marks of antichristic teaching.

Inheritance of the Kingdom

The future participation of God's people in the everlasting reign of Christ. Daniel and Paul both direct the church beyond beastly oppression to the kingdom given to the holy ones.

Institutionalized Apostasy

Apostasy that has developed beyond individual error into organized structures, systems, or offices claiming religious legitimacy while departing from apostolic truth.

Institutionalized Idolatry

The organized public form of false worship, especially as seen in Revelation's image of the beast. It is idolatry made visible, social, and enforceable.

J

Jehovah

The covenant name of God, represented by the Tetragrammaton in the Hebrew Scriptures. In this book, Jehovah is the proper name used for the God of Scripture.

Judgment

God's righteous evaluation and sentencing of individuals, powers, kingdoms, and the whole anti-God order. Prophecy repeatedly teaches that judgment belongs finally to Jehovah through His Messiah.

Judicial Delusion

God's righteous handing over of truth-rejecting people to the deception they have chosen. In 2 Thessalonians 2, those who do not love the truth are given over to believe the lie as an act of divine judgment.

K

Kingdom of God

God's righteous rule manifested through His Messiah. In the prophetic context of this book, it stands in direct contrast to the beastly order and is finally given in open triumph to Christ and the holy ones.

Kingdom of the Beast

The anti-God order of political-religious rebellion that demands allegiance, persecutes the faithful, and is finally destroyed at Christ's coming.

King of Kings

A title given to Jesus Christ in Revelation, emphasizing His supreme sovereignty over every earthly ruler and every rebellious kingdom.

L

Lake of Fire

The final place or symbol of irreversible divine judgment in Revelation. It is the appointed end of the beast, the false prophet, the devil, death, Hades, and all who remain in rebellion against God.

Lamb

A title for Jesus Christ in Revelation that emphasizes His sacrificial death, redemptive worthiness, and final victory. The Lamb is opposed by the beastly order but ultimately conquers all anti-God powers.

Last Hour

John's expression for the climactic age already present in the apostolic period, marked by the activity of many antichrists. It shows that antichrist was not merely future from John's point of view.

Last Things

A broad term for the final events and realities associated with Christ's coming, judgment, resurrection, kingdom, and the destruction of all anti-God powers.

Lawlessness

Rebellion against God's authority, truth, and order. In prophecy, lawlessness is not mere social disorder but self-exalting defiance against divine rule, especially in the realm of worship.

Little Horn

A figure in Daniel representing arrogant, self-exalting, persecuting power. The little horn provides major prophetic background for later descriptions of anti-God dominion, the man of lawlessness, and the beast.

Lying Signs and Wonders

Counterfeit displays of power used by satanic deception to support false worship and false authority. Their purpose is not to confirm truth but to lead people into the lie.

M

Man of Lawlessness

Paul's term in 2 Thessalonians 2 for the concentrated public expression of institutionalized apostate rebellion. He is a religious usurper who exalts himself in the sphere of worship and is destroyed by Christ's appearing.

Mark of the Beast

The sign of allegiance to the beastly political-religious order in thought and action. It is not to be reduced to a shallow technological theory, because Revelation presents it first as a matter of worship, identity, and submission, and only then as a matter of economic coercion.

Messiah

The Anointed One promised in Scripture, fulfilled in Jesus Christ. All antichristic and beastly opposition is ultimately opposition to Jehovah's Messiah and His rightful kingship.

Messianic Rule

The reign of Christ over all nations, enemies, and kingdoms. Scripture presents His rule as righteous, irresistible, and final.

Mystery of Lawlessness

The hidden but already active principle of rebellion Paul says was at work in the apostolic age before the lawless one was fully revealed. It refers to the developing anti-God force operating beneath the surface of history.

N

Name of the Beast

The identifying designation of the beastly order, tied in Revelation 13 to the mark and to the number 666. It signifies belonging to the beast's order and bearing its anti-God identity.

Name of God

The divine name borne by God's servants as a sign of ownership, covenant identity, and holy belonging. It stands in deliberate contrast to the mark and name of the beast.

Nations

The peoples and rulers of the earth considered collectively, especially as they appear in rebellion against Jehovah and His Anointed in Psalm 2, Daniel, and Revelation.

Number of the Beast

The number 666, which interprets the beastly order as the mature expression of fallen humanity in rebellion against God. It is called a man's number because it belongs to man in arrogant independence from Jehovah, not to divine fullness.

O

Object of Worship

Anything honored, revered, or served in the place of God. The lawless one exalts himself above every so-called god or object of worship, making this phrase important for understanding his usurping character.

Overcomers

Believers who remain faithful to Christ despite deception, persecution, and pressure from the beastly order. In Revelation, overcomers share in Christ's victory and inheritance.

P

Parousia

A Greek term often translated "coming" or "presence," especially in reference to Christ's return. In this book's framework, it is tied to the visible triumph of Christ over all anti-God power.

Persecution

Oppression or suffering inflicted upon God's people because of their loyalty to Christ. In Revelation and the Gospels, persecution is one of the defining marks of messianic opposition.

Political-Religious Composite

A description of the anti-God order in Revelation 13, in which beastly political dominion, deceptive religious power, and institutionalized idolatry work together as one coordinated rebellion against God.

Prince of Princes

A Danielic title pointing to the supreme ruler against whom arrogant anti-God powers set themselves. It anticipates the full supremacy of Christ over every rebellious authority.

Public Worship

Open acts of devotion, reverence, and submission. In the final conflict, public worship becomes one of the chief dividing lines between the servants of God and the followers of the beast.

Q

Quickening of Apostasy

The historical acceleration of defection from apostolic truth once restraining apostolic presence is removed. Though not a direct biblical phrase, it describes the progressive exposure of the mystery of lawlessness.

R

Rebellion

Willful resistance to God's authority, truth, and order. In prophecy, rebellion reaches its mature form in apostasy, lawlessness, beast-worship, and the gathering of the nations against Christ.

Redeemed

Those purchased or delivered by God through the sacrifice of Christ. Revelation contrasts the redeemed people of the Lamb with those who belong to the beastly world-order.

Remnant

The faithful people preserved by God in the midst of widespread apostasy or judgment. Revelation 12:17 speaks of the dragon's war against the rest of the woman's offspring, a remnant loyal to God and to Jesus.

Restraint

The act of holding back the full manifestation of the lawless order. In this book's framework, apostolic presence and authority function as a restraining force during the apostolic age.

Restrainer

The force holding back the full manifestation of the lawless one in 2 Thessalonians 2. In the framework of this book, the most coherent understanding is that apostolic presence and authority functioned as that restraint while the mystery of lawlessness was already at work.

Resurrection

God's act of raising the dead. In this theological framework, resurrection is not the release of an immortal soul, but the restoration of life by God's power.

Rod of Iron

A symbol of the Messiah's irresistible and righteous rule over rebellious nations. It comes from Psalm 2 and is applied in Revelation to Christ's final victory over the beastly order.

S

Sacrilege

An act of profaning what belongs to God. The abomination of desolation and the self-exaltation of the lawless one are both forms of sacrilegious rebellion.

Satan

The great adversary of God and His people, also called the devil, the dragon, and the ancient serpent. He is the father of the lie and the unseen source behind the beastly order.

Seal of God

The divine mark of ownership placed upon God's servants, especially in Revelation. It stands in deliberate contrast to the mark of the beast and signifies belonging to Jehovah and the Lamb.

Self-Exaltation

The defining attitude of anti-God rulers and systems in Daniel, Paul, and Revelation. Self-exaltation is the creature's attempt to rise above divine limits and claim authority or worship that belongs only to God.

Seven

A number frequently used in Revelation to signify fullness, completeness, or divinely ordered totality. It provides the symbolic backdrop for understanding why 666 signifies intensified human deficiency and falling short.

Sheol

The grave, the realm of the dead, or gravedom in Hebrew Scripture. In this theological framework, it does not mean conscious torment after death but the condition of death.

Signs and Wonders

Displays of power that can be either true or counterfeit. In the final anti-God order, lying signs and wonders are satanic instruments of deception used to support false worship and rebellion against God.

Son of Destruction

A title Paul gives to the man of lawlessness. It points both to his character and to his destiny, marking him out as one who belongs to ruin and is appointed to divine judgment.

Spirit of Antichrist

The anti-Christ principle already active in the world, according to John. It is expressed in teachings and influences that deny the truth about Jesus Christ.

Spiritual Warfare

The conflict between God's truth and satanic deception, especially as it unfolds through false doctrine, persecution, counterfeit religion, and beastly power.

T

Temple of God

In the context of 2 Thessalonians 2, the sphere claiming relation to God in which the lawless one exalts himself. In this book's argument, it should be understood primarily in connection with religious usurpation rather than a merely secular setting.

Testimony of Jesus

The faithful witness borne concerning Jesus Christ, or the witness given by Him. In Revelation, those who hold the testimony of Jesus are the objects of dragonic hostility.

Theological Rebellion

Revolt against God as He has revealed Himself, especially through false teaching about Christ, false worship, and the rejection of apostolic truth.

Throne

A symbol of ruling authority. Revelation contrasts the throne of God and of the Lamb with the throne and authority given by the dragon to the beast.

Truth

The revealed reality of God in Christ as proclaimed by the apostles. In this book, the decisive issue is not mere possession of information, but love of the truth, because those who reject the truth become vulnerable to deception and judgment.

U

Usurpation

The act of seizing a place, authority, or honor that belongs to another. The lawless and beastly order is usurping because it claims what belongs only to Jehovah and to His Christ, especially in the sphere of worship.

Unclean Spirits

Demonic agents of deception associated in Revelation with the dragon, the beast, and the false prophet. They help gather the kings of the earth for final rebellion.

V

Victory of the Lamb

The triumphant overthrow of every anti-God power by Jesus Christ. This is the final theological center of the book and the proper ending point of all prophetic interpretation.

Visible Profession

Outward identification with the Christian faith without necessarily possessing genuine perseverance in apostolic truth. A major theme of the book is distinguishing visible profession from true biblical Christianity.

W

War Against the Holy Ones

IDENTIFYING THE ANTICHRIST

The repeated prophetic pattern in which beastly powers attack God's people. Daniel, Revelation, and the words of Jesus all show that persecution belongs to the conflict between the kingdom of God and the anti-God order.

Wicked One

A title for the lawless enemy set against God, truth, and the people of God. In 2 Thessalonians 2, the lawless one is ultimately destroyed by Christ's appearing.

Wisdom

Spiritual discernment shaped by God's revelation. In Revelation 13:18, wisdom is required to understand the number of the beast properly rather than sensationally.

Witness

Testimony to the truth of God and of Christ. The faithful witness of believers stands in direct opposition to false prophecy and beastly deception.

Worship

Reverence, submission, and devotion directed toward one recognized as supreme. In Revelation, the central conflict is over worship: whether humanity will worship God and the Lamb, or the dragon, the beast, and its image.

World-Order

The organized human order in rebellion against God. In Revelation, this world-order reaches mature form in the beastly political-religious system.

X

Xenophobia of the Beastly Order

Not a direct biblical term, but useful only with caution if ever used to describe the beast's hostility toward all who refuse conformity. This term is better avoided in the book itself unless carefully qualified.

Y

Yielding to the Lie

The act of embracing deception instead of the truth. In 2 Thessalonians 2, those who do not love the truth are given over to believe the lie.

Z

Zeal for the Truth

Earnest devotion to apostolic doctrine and loyalty to Christ. Such zeal stands opposite the doctrinal indifference that opens the door to apostasy and deception.

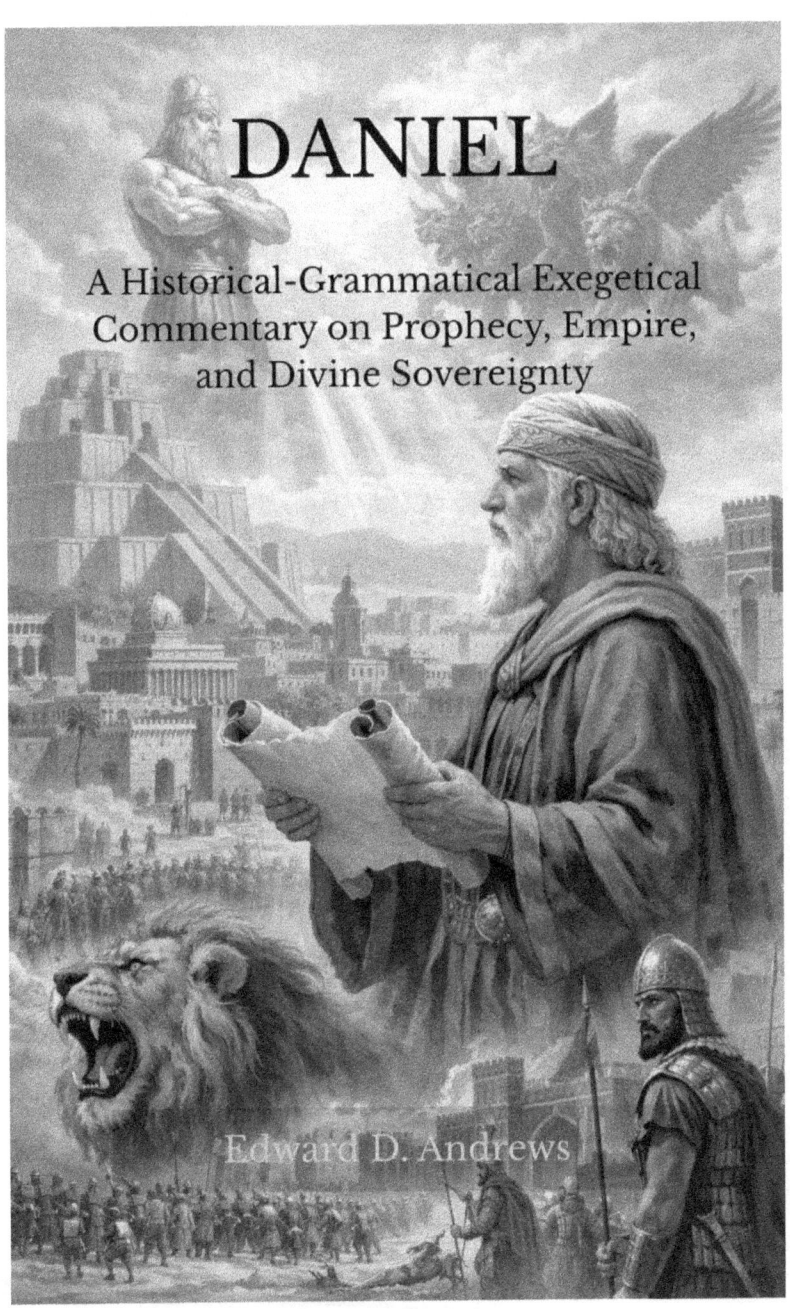

Edward D. Andrews

Bibliography

Akin, D. L. (2001). *The New American Commentary: 1, 2, 3 John*. Nashville, TN: Broadman & Holman.

Aland, K., Black, M., & Martini, C. M. (1993; 2006). *The Greek New Testament, Fourth Revised Edition (Interlinear With Morphology)*. Deutsche Bibelgesellschaft: United Bible Society.

Andrews, E. D. (2023). *BIBLICAL APOCALYPTICS HANDBOOK: A Study of the Most Important Revelations that God and Christ Disclosed in the Bible*. Cambridge, OH: Christian Publishing House.

Andrews, E. D. (2024). *CHRISTIAN THEOLOGY: The Christian's Ultimate Guide to Learning from the Bible*. Cambridge, OH: Christian Publishing House.

Barnes, A. (1884-85). *Barnes On Revelation: Albert Barnes' Notes On The Whole Bible*. London: Blackie & Son.

Collins, ,. J. (1994). *Daniel: A Commentary on the Book of Daniel*. Minneapolis, MN: Fortress Press.

Easley, K. H. (1999). *Holman New Testament Commentary - Revelation (Volume 12)*. Nashville, TN: Broadman & Holman.

Ian, P. (2018). *Revelation: An Introduction and Commentary (Volume 20)*. Downers Grove, Il: InterVarsity Press.

Miller, S. (1994). *Daniel (New American Commentary, 18)*. Nashville, TN: Broadman & Holman Reference.

Thomas, R. L. (1992). *Revelation 1-7: An Exegetical Commentary*. Chicago, IL: Moody Publishers.

Thomas, R. L. (1995). *Revelation 8-22: An Exegetical Commentary*. Chicago, IL: Moody Publishers.

Walvoord, J. F. (2012). *Daniel (The John Walvoord Prophecy Commentaries)*. Chicago, IL: Moody Publishers.